"You are aware prior to birth and aware after you die, so you begin with awareness, but you are not conscious of awareness."

~ Richard Rose

Sense of Self

The Source of All Existential Suffering?

Art Ticknor

TAT Foundation Press

TAT Foundation Press, Hurdle Mills, NC.
Website: *www.tatfoundation.org*.

Cover design: Ike Harijanto & Stephen D'Andrea

Inside cover photo: Atlantic Ocean from Dún Aonghus cliff, Inis Mór (Aran Islands). Photo by author.

Cover fonts: Garamond, Myriad Pro
Text fonts: Palatino Linotype, Amazone BT, Printers Ornaments One, Memoir

Library of Congress Control Number: 2020937178

Publisher's Cataloging-in-Publication data

Ticknor, Art.
Sense Of Self: The Source of all Existential Suffering? / written by Art Ticknor.
p. cm.
Includes index.
ISBN 978-0-9864457-6-7

1. Spirituality. 2. Self-Realization. 3. Philosophy. I. Title.

Table of Contents

Hello, Friend

I used to look down my nose at Western folks who casually tossed *Namaste* around in gesture, vocally, or in closing a written communication. It seemed to me such a prideful display. But I must have mellowed a bit in recent years.

I'd lived in Moundsville, WV, a small city with a population just shy of 10,000, for about 20 years and had put this book together early in 2013 just before moving to Florida—then let it age for half a dozen years before publishing it. I'd begun attending hatha yoga classes a year or two before then. The class was taught in a beautiful new facility in the county park on the hill above the town by the park director's wife, a professor at a nearby university. We would spread our mats in a large circle for the *asanas*, and she would close the hour-long session with us in a final posture, sitting on our mats, by saying "Namaste" to us, which we would then repeat... with a heartfelt sense of community.

The sense of self that develops in us at an early age tells us that we are separate beings, things apart, and we eventually long for an end to that separation. We strive for community, for intimate relationships—and yet we fear losing our separate identity.

The *Urban Dictionary* says that the Sanskrit word Namaste means: "The Spirit within me salutes the Spirit in you, knowing that we are all made from the same One Divine Consciousness." That implication had always seemed glib to me—fluent and voluble but insincere and shallow—since I didn't know if it were true.

After a quarter century of conscious struggle, I discovered what I am at the core of being. And I can now say with conviction that whoever came up with that definition either knew or intuited correctly what they were talking about.

Alone

We're here today
working together
in hopes of accelerating
your return… recycling.

You fear being alone
because it reminds you of something
you don't want to think about:
that we die alone.

Jesus said:
"Many stand before the door,
but it is the Alone
who enters the bridechamber."

The word *alone*
comes from Middle English,
a contraction of
all and *one*.

We are working together
so that you can return
to your true state
of non-separation.

First Scattering of Seeds

I believe that most intentional celibacy results from between-ness—a sort of active state of passivity or surrender while noting our desired preference—following a struggle.

❧

Here's another formula to add to the collection: The path to self-realization is quite simple. All one has to do is play the self-definition game with oneself. Regardless of how the player goes about it, he must see what he believes himself to be and then see contradictory evidence. (Definition requires comparison.[1]) Disillusionment is an iterative process as experience loosens the hold of our faulty self-beliefs.

❧

The only solution to existential suffering may be to find out what you really are. If you can grab onto that lifeline, it may save you from a lifetime of continued misery.

❧

Self-inquiry begins with a question, requires direct looking at the mind, and successively reveals false self-identification. There's no formula for doing this.

❧

---

1   Pithy observation of Richard Rose (see www.TATfoundation.org).

The analytical process in its highest functioning leads to paradox. We can never adequately analyze what to do. Feeling—preferably refined feeling—has to guide our actions (and, if we look, I think we may see that it does)… hopefully moderated by common-sense analysis.

🌾

True commitment, in my experience, isn't twisting our mental arm to do something we don't want to do. It's recognizing what we truly want. When we see and admit to ourselves what we truly want or long for with all our heart, the question of priority, of which master to serve, has been answered.

🌾

Introspecting the mind: Imagine two mirrors facing each other. Now imagine that you're one of those mirrors. Now imagine that you're the other mirror….

🌾

I suspect everyone feels what they truly want, but other desires and fears shut out that "voice of silence." Why else would we be afraid to spend time in solitary retreat without the typical distractions?

🌾

The movie projector is a metaphor for how the Self manifests as mind-self. It's as if our life-experience is a film moving in front of a light source, which projects the moving frames onto a screen, where we see a continuously moving life playing out.

The journey back to Self is a loosening of the hypnotic spell with the life-play we're watching. As we're able to take in more and more of the mind movement, it's as if we were backing up the projected ray of light. Eventually the hypnotic spell breaks entirely, and we find ourselves back in full recognition of what we truly are.

What keeps you from admitting that you are what you're looking for?

The only escape hatch [from being identified with the infinite loop of the mind] is back through awareness to Awareness.

Effort is relative to the "viewing platform" we're observing from. It has nothing to do with what's going on. When attention is close to the hoe, hoeing is effortful. The same goes for meditation. Life is effortful in close-up, effortless in far-shot.

God seems to be hidden only because we can't admit the truth of what we see without seeing through our faulty beliefs about what we are.

If our True Self is entirely free of matter, it is a Perfect Vacuum. If we aren't consciously one with that Perfect Vacuum Self, then we must be, or must be identified with, a space containing matter... and there must be a "door" separating the two. If it's possible to become consciously one with the True Self, the door must open.

Mohiniyattam dance performance—Namaste gesture

First Songs of Self

Question & answer correspondence:

Solid Ground of Being—the perfect book for any level of seeker. Chapter brevity allows time to attack the offending problem, before wordiness has a chance to become obsessive thought.

The core message of your thoughts, your ideas—are obviously not yours, but free to anyone for the taking. But "I" cannot reach the fruit, that is the dilemma.

"Control" pg 22. Your friend who resolved to do anything the guru told him...

I cringed inside. I can think of a great many things I would not like to be told to do. If my secrets were exposed... oh my... the shame, the embarrassment.

I want that thing gone. Like a parasite attacking its host. "If thy eye offend thee, pluck it out" Where does one find the will to pluck out an eye?

Plucking out the eye that offends would probably be a case of how the mind-self splits into two (like everything else in the mind)... Alfred Pulyan referred to them as ego-1 and ego-2, Hubert Benoit termed them saint and sinner. We see one set of characteristics that support the self image that we want to believe ourselves to be or at least to project for others to believe, and another set of characteristics that contradict the ideal self image.

For example, I always told myself I'd rather take a bullet (figuratively, at least :-) rather than see a friend hurt. But one time I'd been doing a roofing job on the Rose farm with a friend... it was toward the end of the day, and we were tired and irritable. I said something to him, he replied in a cutting way (I no longer recall the details), and I immediately said something cutting back to him. That evening and for most of the next day I felt mentally nauseous... due to my self-image taking a hit.

There are habits and addictions that we can see are harmful to ourselves or others and that we may wish to inhibit, but the way to do that isn't with a scalpel. We see behavior patterns that we don't like playing out, and we determine that we'll react differently the next time the situation arises. With sufficient determination and experimentation, the behavior can be inhibited. That reaction to react differently in the future, when it's successful, is what we accurately label as "will."

I found that acceptance is magical and that we don't have to like a characteristic in order to accept it... and once we accept it (the truth of an addiction, for example) our behavior is more likely to change. The secrets we feel we need to hide are precisely what keep us identified with the make-believe self.

Glad you like the book. Your comments would make a good addition to the handful of reviews on Amazon and on Barnes & Noble websites.

Please excuse the lame book review. After an untold number of discarded drafts, I gave up, and just entered some impersonal sentences to finish the job.

I'm utterly frustrated. And immensely sad. Not sure where I go from here.

Think I'll disappear for a while, and withdraw into myself even further.

Thank you for all of your time, it was greatly appreciated.

The review was great, Dan. Thanks. (I think you're being a bit hard on yourself :-)

The body-mind self is like a child... it needs love and encouragement.

Frustration is healthy. Sadness is noteworthy, something to feel deeply. Once we've experienced something fully, we don't need to re-experience it. Every experience carries a message in my opinion... not a particle of life experience is wasted. It's like a teacher who continues trying to get our attention and keep it long enough to help us learn. Every student is different in his capability and inclination to pick up a lesson. As students of life we swallow the lessons at the speed we're able to.

The best position for getting a better view usually comes from leaning in the opposite direction from the one we've been leaning in. For someone who habitually tries to keep distracted by immersing himself in social activities, some alone time can work wonders. For someone who tends to avoid people and social interaction, a little more of that can be helpful. The path to self-knowing is contra-ego... our personality having formed largely as a defensive mechanism to protect faulty beliefs.

※

These days, I have the impression that meditating has done nothing for me. Yesterday I sat for 15 or 20 minutes, lost in thought about gutter and video problems before I remembered (Oh!) that I had sat to meditate. Oh well. "It was worth a try."

Lots of underlying anger these days also, wanting to scream and put my fist through walls and toilet stalls. Somewhat frustrated you might say, with the continuing, persisting delusion of self.

I remember getting to the point after about 20 years where I felt like I was right back where I'd started. Friends could see that wasn't the case, but it sure seemed that way to me.

The body-mind self is real enough, like a bus is real enough. The *belief* in "no self" seems absurd to me. What ends our existential suffering is when the channel opens between the body-mind self and the core or source of its being. Then we know that what we are, the essential, core self, is beyond the problems of things that exist (i.e., that come and go).

How do we wake up in the morning? Some confluence of events occurs, some of which the body-mind can participate in setting into motion, like setting the alarm clock. If we sleepily turn the alarm off without being conscious of it, we may be angry at ourselves for oversleeping, and that can crank up our determination to be more conscious of what we're doing when semi-awake... which is probably preferable to a reaction of long-suffering sadness at our inability to control things.

Is it possible to experience lasting presence without a realization taking place?

Douglas Harding believed it was possible to get an instantaneous glimpse of what we are at the center and then to practice attaining the glimpse more and more often until it becomes permanent. But how would you know if what you experienced was permanent? Would you be measuring it by consciousness, which comes and goes? I think you'd have to take it on faith. If you're looking for permanence, and what you experience doesn't last, I'd say it's not what you're looking for. On the other hand, I'd say we always see the truth of what we aren't but don't admit or accept the implications. The bottom line may be that experience isn't sufficient. Experience requires a subject-object split, and in the subject-object cosmos the subject is never the known. Since the knower of experience isn't known, there can be no certainty here... only varying probability.

❧

What would allow the realization to sink in deep enough for the fictitiousness of the "Augie" character to be seen through permanently?

I don't have an explanation for it. I felt like there was help, that something lined things up in a way that Art couldn't have done. In any case, when the necessary alignment occurs, we'd have to "see" (intuit) that there's nothing left to hold onto. That could come in a concentrated period as it apparently did for Ramana Maharshi at age 16[2] or over an extended period of years or a lifetime. We don't know whether the length of that period is predetermined or flexible. We don't know if the length of time is influenced by our "actions" (reactions) or the actions/reactions of others. There's not much we know for sure, is there. We play possibilities, we feel the longing for Home, and we witness the war between the desire to sleep and to really awaken. And we alternately struggle and surrender.

❧

---

2   From the preface of *The Collected Works of Ramana Maharshi*, edited by Arthur Osborne

There's something about doing the Harding exercises with eyes closed that bypasses the whole "I'm pointing at my nose!" argument. So, I've been meditating with eyes closed, asking myself if I'm awake/conscious/existent/present, and then asking where "I" am. There seems to be the initial "looking" or whatever you wanna call the reaction to "are you awake?" followed by my mind bouncing into activity. And then I eventually remember to ask again, repeat cycle. With repeated asking and looking, does it eventually become possible to "see" more of what's going on back there? The look after "are you awake?" is so quick at this point, that I haven't been able to tell much about what it is that's even happening after/when I ask the question or what I'm seeing.

I think that the entire trip Home could be described as intuitional seeing and that each person's experience of the expansion of intuition's view will be different. In my case I'd say that seeing "more of what's going on back there" didn't occur until the final hour, and even then it was still the mind's seeing—and specifically the dawning that awareness is self-aware. The implications of that seeing finally untied mind's moorings. There's no eye "back there," but the open channel to the mind provides the necessary mirroring to get a dumbed-down view of ourselves in the reflecting pool of the mind. Maybe. :-) Any attempt to describe "back there" becomes convoluted and misleading. And no view within the mind can really give a preview.

❧

Are you looking for that of you which may be eternal?

On a broad scale, yes, and that knowledge would change self-esteem based on anything impermanent, even if unquestionably oblivion were my eternal, ultimate state. On that scale of really looking, am

I looking for that? I don't really look, mostly I spin about reducing fear so I can look, and occasionally I'll ask in some form and start waiting with some degree of a listening attention, but my patience, or tolerance of that tension doesn't last long enough for anything to get through (consciously anyway, though possibly unconsciously). Even remembering to try again now, the mind doesn't want that tension of even a moment of serious asking. In that sense I lack any real vector of looking for that which may be eternal.

In this sense then my evaluation of myself possibly has no grounding, except as mimed habit. Doesn't sink in through my thick skull.

Oblivion is the opposite of consciousness and equally impermanent. Your conclusion about your self-evaluation having no solid point of reference is accurate. The mind can find its way to the doorway to eternality by what it loves. What we love will eventually provide the necessary confronting of truth vs. non-truth.

Wondering about what I love doesn't take up much of my thinking. Probably just a little of that, as opposed to the endless chain of focus on fear or problems, would bring the mind to the doorstep. It just never does that—it prefers the story of "injured."

Running away from fear is running toward security, toward invulnerability.

Invulnerability does play a role in what I'd hope to find in the truth, as this ego feels so vulnerable so much of the day. The main drama keeping the mind's attention has more to do with vulnerability than imposing the ego on the world. Whether the "I" is as vulnerable as felt (while intellectually unlikely, is still possible, after all, experience appears to back that feeling up) the mind can't find any other candidate for identity besides it, imaginary though it may be from JJ van der Leeuw's perspective[3] (like a table is still only a thought in the experience, as a thought, "me" may not represent the thing in itself). While the subtractive path works better than visualizing stuff, is there another candidate for identity? Preferably that has invulnerability? Perhaps a triangulation could occur.

Invulnerability is an absolute condition, not a candidate for relative transcendence by triangulation. Possible candidates for a final triangulation might be self vs. no self, or life vs. death. The description that Arthur Osborne gave of Venkataraman Iyer's (later to be known as Ramana Maharshi) self-realization was an example of such a triangulation. It always comes back to an investigation into self… and the fact that definition requires comparison.

Did you play hide-and-seek when you were a kid? The game begins by running away and hiding, hoping not to get caught. But the payoff is finding our way back to the home base and touching it before whoever is "it" calls us "out." Can you imagine the possibility of your game-play switching from run-and-hide to going-for-home?

❧

Do you think the fears that arise from the consciousness of physical death are the same ones that block the death of the false self?

No, I think what blocks the death of the false self is pride. Fear of physical death could be a potent reason to investigate the mystery of coming into and going out of existence.

I feel so much of my pride has fallen away, seeing what my life has become. Is any remaining pride just a front for the control that

---

3   *The Conquest of Illusion*

constitutes the will to live? Is it something else I have to uncover so it doesn't covertly continue its blocking? Or is it something that can only be taken from me?

Pride gets more refined and tougher to spot as our quest progresses. The unchanging symptom of pride is that we don't yet admit the truth of what we are. The verb form implies to congratulate oneself. It's reflexive, like Harding's first-person view... and therefore eccentric (off center, not coming from the center or core). Pride is the offspring of being identified with what we witness, with an implied counterpart to experience... i.e., *an* experiencer.

❧

Regarding pride: I think I have some variant of "wanting to surrender on my own terms." In other words, I want to ensure that surrendering would not make my situation any worse.

Occasionally, when I have the mental strength and am feeling generally optimistic, I "want to see how this life turns out before giving it up" (a variant of Richard Rose's daughter telling him spiritual stuff was not for her because she had games to play) which also feels like a pride.

At other times, for instance when I recently re-read a Rumi poem I like and was very moved by it, I can sense that the pride temporarily lessened. And I can sense that moments without pride are greater than moments with pride. So is there something I can do or think of, when I feel pride, that will reduce the pride or remind me to move away from it?

Pride is based on faulty beliefs about what we are. Another way to say it would be that it's based on identification with what we have vs. accurate identification with what we are.

(That's what *becoming,* or *becoming one with,* refers to. We don't become one with something other.) The only way to move away from pride is to see through a faulty self-belief.

Surrender is bowing to the truth of what we are vs. believing picture book fairy tales about it. If we want to know the truth, we let the truth know… and it will bind back upon itself. "If a man sincerely prays and hears himself, he will acquire," as Richard Rose phrased it.

❧

The question of the 'optimal practice' keeps holding court in my head. For some reason I cannot make up my mind and stick to something for a period of time. I think it has to do with control (of the ego over my spiritual progress), not feeling sure about true spiritual practice and fear of making a decision. I feel stuck in this. What can I do?

Go back to basics. Simplify. Really simplify. One thing.

I also see ever more ways in which a belief of not being good enough (negative self-esteem) is an obstacle. But this one is very sticky. What to do?

It's part of the story-of-J that the mental machinery (in the left hemisphere of the brain, per Jill Bolte Taylor) is making up as part of carrying on with its program. It's sticky because the machinery is programmed to feel lost without it. (Are you what you experience/witness?)

❧

Is love more than just a feeling?

If we're talking about the experience of love, I guess all experience comes in the form of thoughts (words, pictures) and feelings (including moods and conviction states).

There are momentary *satoris* of love—being shot by Cupid's arrow—sometimes in the form of romantic love, sometimes a salvation-type experience such as when I fell in love with my infant son.

There are specific feelings or composite thoughts/feelings we describe as feeling love. They're often triggered by embracing someone, making prolonged eye contact, etc.—various forms of rapport. And more abstract forms, such as seeing something that strikes us as beautiful.

Beyond experience is True, Complete Love. Once we wake up to That, we can put experiential love into perspective.

Perhaps all love results from a dropping of defenses. Being "hit" with love is a passive reaction of the mind's being caught off guard, whereas a conscious dropping of defenses is a more active reaction.

Mike L. was telling me about this technique of Rose's that you mentioned to him.

I read [Paul Constant's] entry[4] on Turning the Head, it appears to be just returning to no mind during meditation being interrupted by a thought.

Mike's take on it....

> *I've started an experiment this week after some discussion with Art. I'm trying to institute Rose's procrastination meditation technique each afternoon. I'm not sure if you are familiar with it but the basic premise is to use procrastination for us instead of the way it's usually used against us. I've been doing a seated*

---

4   In the April 2010 *TAT Forum* e-zine, www.tatfoundation.org/forum.htm

or driving meditation and watch my thoughts. When a thought arises that is irrelevant to understanding the inner working of my mental processes, I basically take the stance of putting off thinking about it and direct my attention away from it. Undoubtedly another thought soon comes into the picture, but if it is irrelevant to any greater understanding or any new ideas of how to tackle this whole thing, then I look away from it as well.

Is that all there is to it?

Have you looked into Rose's "Meditation" booklet or *Psychology of the Observer*? They go into his recommendations for going within... a way of holding your head.

Rose described the technique that Mike mentions as "learning to turn the inner head at will." It's not an attempt to turn to some manufactured state of no-thought or no-mind... it's learning to turn the head away from what's not relevant to one's main goal (whatever that is for the person... anywhere on the pyramid of Maslow's hierarchy of aims/games).

Rose described meditation as productive thinking.

Perhaps that's what we're trying to do in our e-mail confrontation group....

❧

Complaint: "I know for sure You are so close by. And yet, you won't let me reach out and touch You" feeling.

Ben R. and I were discussing this at the Monday meeting in Pittsburgh and at the coffee shop afterward... that feelings are facts, but the mind's interpretation of a feeling is subject to scrutiny. And the mind seems programmed to look for data that support its interpretation of any feeling rather than for contradictory data. Yet, from a viewpoint above the problem, the opposite interpretation is equally valid. Not surprisingly when we consider it, the mind gravitates toward the less painful or less disconcerting side of the coin. You consider "your" interpretation to be painful, but what if you looked for data that supports the opposite belief... which might be something along the line of: "the feeling tells cap-m *Me* that small-y *you* are so close by (right here, actually) and *I* am touching *you* all the time, yet *you* don't admit it"?

❦

I suspect if my general level of motivation in life were better, this problem [aimless web searching, napping, etc.] would likely disappear by itself.

Where do you suspect higher levels of motivation come from?

I have no clue. My general belief is, all motivations come from the need of the animal to survive and reproduce. Pursuing the Truth to avoid death is therefore understandable, but I'm baffled by why I even very occasionally feel what I think/am told is the love of god, because this seems like something outside the sphere of the animal. Either way, I sense resignation in answering your question: I feel like saying "Well, I don't know. Either I have motivation, or I don't. If I don't, I'll continue on my current life trajectory, and eventually die. If I do, I'll pursue a higher cause, and maybe it'll pay off."

Suppose finding what you're looking for is like getting to the end of a long story or like drinking an inordinately large smoothie, and the duration of your quest corresponds to the speed at which you're willing or able to imbibe the less tasty parts. And suppose that you intuit that what you're looking for is capital-r Rest... but that you love life despite (or maybe because of) its ups and downs, and you're afraid that Rest = death = end of life/love. Where would the motivation come from to speed up the page turning or gulp swallowing?

❧

Was listening to your latest video at the SIG meeting and was curious about something. When you said you were depressed for 7 years after Richard Rose did not reply to your letter, did you ever see him again?

Yes. :-) The shock occurred at the end of 1989 or beginning of 1990. In the middle of 1991 I moved from Miami, Florida to the Rose farm in WV in order to keep it available for people to use for solitary retreats in cabins scattered in the woods on the property, which hadn't been farmed in decades. Rose and his wife and daughter lived on the farm during the summer months, when school was out. I'd brought my mother up from Miami with me—after having relocated her there from her home in NY a couple of years earlier— and she was living in the town where Rose lived during the school year, where he or his wife could check in on her if I got snowed in at the farm. I felt like I needed to check her every day since she wasn't taking good care of herself and wasn't overly cooperative with women I'd have come in to help her. She went into a nursing home in 1996, after which I did my first solitary retreat since 1989. During the retreat I had a revelation that ended the depression.

❧

"The content of the mind doesn't matter." [From Art's statement to D: "Do you remember Richard, the older guy who comes to the Pgh meetings from Akron OH? When Tess came to the meeting on Oct. 10th, she said something to him after he finished a complex, analytical exposition about his situation. She said: 'The content of the mind isn't important.' Do you see how that could be true?"]

It doesn't matter...unless it does.

Sorry to hear that this is as far as you can run with it....

It amazes me that I have the energy to run any distance with these questions. You'd think I would've run out of gas years ago. My flippant response was a byproduct of my recent obsession with paradoxes. The statement "the content of the mind doesn't matter" is paradoxical because, if true, then it doesn't matter. It could only matter if it isn't true. But if it isn't true, then the statement should hardly matter to us. Yet, it seems quite important. Are you feeling the absurdity? I am. The whole world has an undercurrent of absurdity, right down to my sense of self.

Nope... it may be incongruous or unreasonable, but it doesn't strike me as ridiculously or foolishly so. Maybe that's because I know that what we are is beyond paradox. I suspect your proclivity toward complexity helps you avoid the possible threat that the statement may imply: In the final transition beyond paradox, the "you" you believe yourself to be will be left behind.

❧

I am at the point that I will not ever know for certain what I am, only what I am not. That leaves me bouncing somewhere between awareness and awareness of awareness. It feels like Awareness of Awareness is the seer? Am I on track with that?

How is it that I can be awareness but not be the seer?

There's thinking... feeling... and looking.

Thinking postulates what we are, based on what we've heard, read, observed. Feeling indicates where to look. Looking automatically shows us when what we see (intuit) is at odds with what we believe. We don't want to "see" what we see if it contradicts beliefs, since that would rock the boat of our minimal security.

It's an iterative process of noticing what we're thinking and feeling... and seeing.

I'm having trouble feeling again. Feeling used to be my strong point, but I beat it out of me to be more logical.

Feeling feelings is very simple. It's merely noticing what we're already feeling. The intellect adds a layer of complication trying to interpret the message of the feeling.

※

I'm thinking about committing to focus the next 4 months on the following:

- *Watch the mind*
- *Feel the longing*
- *Train the mind to be less distracted by problems other than self-definition.*

From what I got from our conversation, the first is the most important, the basic spiritual practice. The second is something I could start my meditation with (I'm thinking about setting aside an hour a day for watching the mind, and starting with connecting to the longing. The first point is actually something I can do all day, but to dedicate an hour specifically seems like a good idea). The third one is something to be aware of, but I don't have any specific practice in mind. Just to keep these 3 things in mind will be more than enough. What do you think about this approach?

I'd suggest trying to simplify it in your mind even more, J. You want to get a feeling for what it encompasses without having to refer to notes, etc. Not that keeping a short, written reminder of it isn't a good idea, too.

The main thing is to remember why you're doing it... the life-objective you're trying to accomplish. In my case, the words that rang the bell for me were "to become the Truth at any cost." A couple of times I found subtitles, such as "to obey the Lord in thought, word and deed," but these were additional facets of the words that described my deep longing. Actually feeling the longing is powerful medicine.

Meditation, then, is training the mind to focus on the objective... by turning its attention away from distractions and irrelevancies.

PS: It's not "J. watching the mind" as much as it's the mind consciously watching the objects (thoughts, feelings, pictures, smells, etc.) passing in front of it.

⚜

Looking more into the fear I talked about the last night [of the retreat] I see that this is not fear of death, which seems to be a big problem to most people. It is more a fearful child in an adult's body. An insecurity—fear of being left out, being expelled. I do not know if it is an unnecessary step to find out what the feeling is/is about to find out that I am not that feeling. Is this just making another story being added to the long row that I am already sick of?

Fear of death wasn't a big motivator for me, either. When I read one time about the term "hell" being associated with the place where transgressors lived who were shunned from Jerusalem (the valley of Gehenna) and where they had to survive by scavenging food from the city dump, I realized that was exactly what all my social fears came down to: being cast out of the city. Every time someone frowns at us or criticizes us, or we're in an embarrassing situation, etc., if we feel it deeply, it leads us all the way back to the fear of annihilation. We can't conceive of what that would be, but we have some emotional picture or feeling of what it means to us.

I don't know that it's necessary to understand feelings, although my mentality always liked to have words to put with them. But feelings, I believe, are designed for the organism's survival long enough to fulfill its purpose. So their message is one of "move toward, grab" or "move away, let go." The deepest feeling, the longing for Home, falls into the "move toward" category. It's not something we can grab, however. Moving toward Home is a "backing toward" process, although in a way it may be like tacking a sailboat since the wind of life seems to be coming from there.

It may be sufficient to consciously feel feelings and let the mind interpret their possible message.

❧

Does the organism have a purpose to fulfill? Do you know the purpose of yours?

I didn't question my purpose until I was getting ready to graduate from college. Then I went through periodic identity crises over the next dozen years, feeling that something was missing in my life (purpose, meaning) but not being able to get a hook into what it was. Then I met Richard Rose, and when I heard him say that the answers are within, I felt like I'd found my purpose... which was self-definition/self-realization/becoming the Truth.

I think purpose is dynamic, manifesting as action. In retrospect, someone at our funeral can assume that whatever we did was our de facto purpose. I no longer question my purpose, nor do I pray (as it would be a bit schizophrenic :-) but I think both are valuable actions while we're undefined.

❧

Tension is a subject that is hard for me to get a grip on. I get that the friction between being awareness and being aware of that creates helpful tension. But there is also the tension of many unresolved old issues and when I release some of it through for example a cathartic emotional cleansing, I feel afterward more energy and clarity. So there seems to be tension that is helpful and tension that better be resolved. What is your opinion about tension? What is productive and what is unproductive tension (in the context of the search)?

Tension comes from the tug of opposites. Life is tension. Productive tension is anything that results in turning the inner head away from distraction. Productive tension is anything that enhances intuition. Productive tension is anything that generates a reaction to react differently the next time an undesirable pattern begins to play out.

When I observe myself there is usually an immediate reaction to it. When for example I suddenly become aware that I'm completely identified with a daydream, the daydream stops immediately. But to my understanding the idea is that one observes without changing the view. Yet with daydreams (or other thoughts) that seems particularly difficult. Do you have a suggestion?

There may be times when daydreaming is productive. If there's something else that you're trying to accomplish at the time, then procrastinate the daydreaming until a more appropriate time. Conscious observation—i.e., noticing what we're seeing—may affect what we see.

How do you know that enlightenment isn't just a conviction state?

What form of proof would you find acceptable? (Seriously.) Don't settle for any "enlightenment" that isn't a form of knowing that's different from any type of knowing you've experienced.

"Becoming"

I descended
from the Impersonal
into the personal...
Why?
To experience
something.

I struggled to arise
from the personal...
Why?
To answer the call
from within
to return home.

I descended once again
from the Impersonal...
Why?
It's always about Love

    becoming love
             becoming Love.

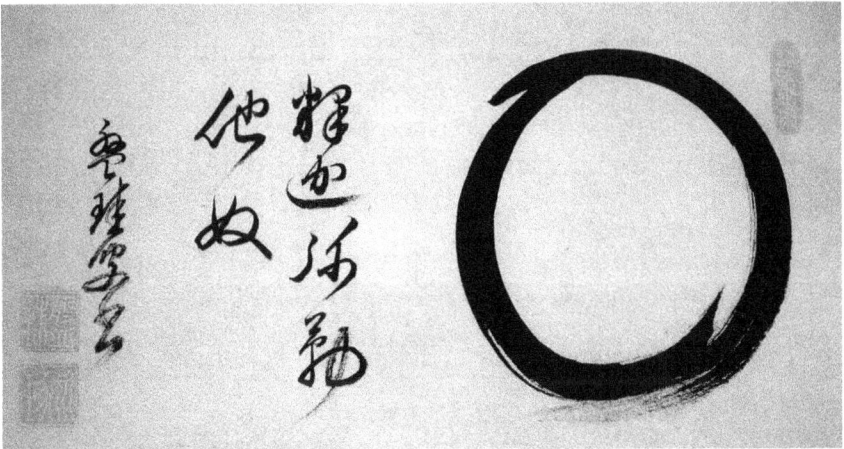

Bankei's *ensō: The Unborn Buddha Mind*

More Birdseed

If you can buy these assumptions for the sake of investigation, what's your feeling about who or what is currently holding the door shut?

※

Incarnation in a body-mind brings the ability to know *that* you *are* (i.e., self-consciousness). *What* you are can't be completely seen or encompassed by the body-mind. What's your strategy for escaping the limitations of the body-mind's view?

※

Searching for the center? The center is where you are... always.

※

The perspective that "settles our soul" is not one that comes from what we see when looking outward but what we find by looking/going inward... before and beyond seer and seen.

※

It's amazing how much suffering we "demand" before being moved to acceptance and then from acceptance to a final surrender—acceptance of what we're not and surrender to what we are.

The sticking point is always what you know. At some point you'll need to put everything you think you know off to the side. Reading won't do it, recalling the words of the gurus won't do it. Your seeing will have to become its own authority.

God the True Mother-Father is always saying: "Come home and all will be well." We hear it when we turn our attention to it—our deep longing. We court distraction, though, intuiting that we're not yet ready. As Richard Rose's step-daughter said to him after she read *The Albigen Papers*, "I know you're God… but I still have games to play." When we're ready to respond to the call of our deep longing with all our heart, we find the way.

Are you looking for that of you which may be eternal?

Beliefs are like tranquilizers. Strong beliefs are like sleeping pills.

Some convictions are enslaving, some freeing. Trust in the relative fails us. Trust in the absolute eventually frees us.

To know the knower, there can't be any split between knower and known.

If you're dissatisfied, there's a question or problem you're wrestling with or maybe trying to avoid wrestling with. Underlying that dissatisfaction is some belief or set of beliefs that are being threatened. Satisfaction lies in bringing those beliefs into view, where the light of awareness can show their limitations.

Working with others for help in seeing through faulty beliefs relies on revealing our thoughts and feelings in order to get reactions that may help expose those beliefs to the light of awareness.

Happiness is relative and most relative to recent experience. Happiness is: when the elephant gets up after he's been sitting on you. Would you like to get beyond happiness and unhappiness?

We have everything that's necessary at every instant. We *are* what we're looking for. The truth is not an object but the subject we tell ourselves is searching for it.

Richard Rose said it all when he said: "I'm always right behind you [the "I" referring to the real Self]."

We don't have to wait for Huang Po to shout his MU!!!!!!! that sent disciples into non-sensory awareness ("deafened") for three days.

The preliminary is getting serious about investigating—by looking at—what we believe ourselves to be. Eventually that leads us to direct looking, and direct looking leads to the breakthrough.

❧

Oblivion is the opposite of consciousness and equally impermanent. The mind can find its way to the doorway to eternality by what it loves. What we love will eventually provide the necessary confronting of truth vs. non-truth.

❧

Desire-voices tell us to run toward something; fear-voices tell us to run away. Stress releases cortisol into the bloodstream; cortisol tells the survival program: "fight or flee."

When you're not emotionally turbulent, you might take a look at what you're running from or what the fear/flee voice is trying to protect.

More Songs

*S*o, *I know that this question is not a good use of my time (or yours) and that it will lead me no closer to the Truth, and you may reject it and tell me that I should probably be looking at the question itself if I want to get anywhere—you're right—but I'm curious, so here goes: in your daily existence, how often do you recognize that you are the Truth, or is it a constant companion? Or stated another way, how often are you so lost in the day's activity that you don't notice that you Are, or is there a constant recognition?*

The best I can describe it, John, is that whenever the question comes up—or you could say whenever the need arises—Art's mind is reassured. I can't testify that it would always be the case... for example, if a hemorrhagic stroke or Alzheimer's affects the brain's operation. The mind, or Art's mind, doesn't repeat an endless chant of "I am the Truth" and doesn't feel the need to. It has no concerns about the situation it finds itself in. It knows that true certainty doesn't exist in its domain, but it has an open channel to Me. It has found what every human being, I believe, is looking for. And the finding is worth any cost. (I'm not asking for donations.) :-)

✣

Acceptance & Intuition

I've been thinking a lot about acceptance, especially after talking about it at the last PSI meeting. I noticed that the things that I couldn't accept about myself or my situation are because they are associated with painful/negative emotions. So I asked if I'd change them if I could. The emotional answer coming back kept being a strong "Yes, dummy! Why would you want to feel bad??" It occurred to me at some point that I'd had experiences in the past that were painful, but that I'm glad I went through them in retrospect because I grew from them or learned from them. I wouldn't have chosen to go through those things if I knew up front that they'd be painful, but I wouldn't change the fact that I went through them. And it hit me that I'm not in a position to say that I won't feel the same way in the future about a current painful situation. I'm not in a position to know if the discomfort I'm feeling now might or might not be leading to something I'd be thankful for. And since I don't have the perspective to know that, I've found myself more reluctant to say I'd change anything that's happened to me. I can still see things that I don't like about myself, or that I'd want to do differently if in a similar situation in the future, but I'm not so sure that I'd change the fact that they have happened.

This sense doesn't apply as much to things that are happening externally though. There's a very strong sense of non-acceptance having to do with horrible things people do to each other (torture, rape, etc). I can't rethink the whole world in a way to make those things not exist, but I certainly can't emotionally say I wouldn't change them if I could. Thinking about your feedback for me from the retreat (Feel the difference between here and home), my home is not where those things are. But I can't see anywhere else to go. I hear a loud inner "voice" telling me that going inward as a reaction is a form of escapism and doesn't actually save me.

I don't know if this is the case, Ben, but from your wording, it sounds like you were considering the issue in a general sense. Did you write down the five, say, most painful ones? Did you pick the first item and consider deeply the implications of changing it if you had the power to do so? And then do the same with the 2nd, etc.? Maybe consider the list as if it were someone else's... or construct a list that you believe represents painful characteristics or past experiences for someone else and consider those?

Acceptance doesn't have anything to do with liking or approving. Regarding "external" events... what do you know that the Creative Principle doesn't? Would you abolish all horrible things that people do to each other if you were in charge? Do you know enough to run the universe better than it's currently running? Is it a situation like mine was with deciduous trees? I didn't like the looks of them and thought God had made an ugly choice. I wasn't really concerned about the world or the trees... it was a personal offense to my limited aesthetic. It gets a little more personal when something bad happens to someone we love. We certainly don't have to like it or approve of it or strive to be nonjudgmental of it or of our reactions. Acceptance has to do with an attitude of objectively assessing this organism's capabilities, the limitations of this limited self that we're identified with (and therefore believe ourselves to be). To get into this in any depth, though, we have to get down to simple specifics.

The issue, when you stop to think about it, isn't really with the world at all, is it? Isn't the issue with self and its reactions and discontents?

Regarding "I hear a loud inner 'voice' telling me that going inward as a reaction is a form of escapism and doesn't actually save me": Is that intuition or is it superego, the product of conditioning? If intuition is telling you that you're running away from something, then common sense should take a look at it. If it's a psychological fear, maybe it's worth facing; if it's a physical fear, maybe not. (I don't think the demarcation is necessarily that simple, but maybe you get the gist of what I'm trying to say.)

If we truly believe that something "out there" is going to save us—by which I assume you mean satisfy our deep wanting, I don't see how we can afford not to find out. Disappointment and disillusionment may be the coin of spiritual progress. Caveat emptor.

I haven't been as specific as looking through a list of the top five. How would you go about honestly considering the implications of changing something specific? It's hard to imagine just what would be affected by any specific change. Which maybe in itself is an argument for why I shouldn't be in charge, but that seems to get glossed over emotionally, and my mind holds fast to the idea that things would probably be better even though I can't imagine exactly how. Wishful thinking fills in the gaps.

I could certainly be more specific with "externals" as well. My feeling seems to exist on a very general level as far as atrocities of the world, since I haven't been in direct contact with war/torture/ etc.

This struck a chord:

> The issue, when you stop to think about it, isn't really with the world at all, is it? Isn't the issue with self and its reactions and discontents?

You're right... the issue is mine. The world doesn't have a problem with itself. The issue is the feeling reaction I have to the world and the place I believe I have in it. I feel like there's a very strong conditioned voice telling me that it's irresponsible and selfish to not want to help "save" or "fix" the world. I feel defenseless against this voice because I don't have much argument against it. I don't like the fact that there is human trafficking, and the voice says "so why am I not doing anything about it?" (Same could be said about any other issue.) I answer back that I can't take responsibility for the world, and the conditioned voice says "the least you could do is try." It's overwhelming, all the problems that I would want to fix. Maybe this is where looking at specifics could be a good exercise.

The voice calling going within "escapism" is related to this fix-the-world voice. Going within is a selfish move, born out of giving up on handling the external world and helping to solve its problems, according to this voice. It's clear to me that it's a conditioned voice, and it's not hard to find examples of that social conditioning in everyday life. But it's still hard to shake... I can see it carrying more weight in decision-making than I'd like. It seems to periodically shift the focus of my attention onto the external world, and creates feelings of guilt, loneliness, and something's-wrong-with-me when I don't go along with what seems to be the voice of the culture. (I feel responsible to explain why I'm not doing normal external world activities like dating, starting a family, working on a career, having some sort of hobby passion, doing "socially conscious" activities, etc.)

Something else in me says getting distance from the conditioning is a matter of remembering the feeling of what's really lacking and what I really want. I think that's your voice. I feel like it's easier said than done. My internal landscape doesn't seem clear enough to get a trustworthy sense of what I really want.

How would you go about honestly considering the implications of changing some generality—like deciduous trees or humanity's inhumanity to man?

I think we have to drill down into specifics to get a better look. And I wasn't honestly interested in eliminating deciduous trees from the "external" world (i.e., the images in my mind). I was honestly interested in ending "my suffering." What did my suffering consist of? The repercussions of my conviction that I was affected *in a very specific way* by what I experienced: that what I experienced threatened my welfare and existence.

There may be a vast difference between the do-gooder and a Good Samaritan. The former may be someone who dedicates his life to providing clean drinking water for impoverished villagers and finds that the results of years of effort have elevated the villagers' problems from survivable health problems to terminal mercury poisoning, as I read about resulting from a U.N. program a few years back. The latter may be someone who reacts to a neighbor or a stranger in need of an inconvenient drink of water.

We need to know the truth of a situation in order to try our best for "right action" in any situation. It's one thing to try to determine what may actually help a stranger or a family member who's asking for, or apparently in need of, help. As we get to know our own psychology better, we may be able to step out of the picture enough to get a fairly objective evaluation. Even then, though, right action is problematic. What happens when we elevate our sights to fixing a "big" problem such as world hunger? Who's going to argue that world hunger isn't a problem worth fixing? Bill Gates is devoting billions of dollars to fixing that problem. But the son Howard, of his best friend, Warren Buffett, is trying to convince him that his approach is doomed to failure, temporarily raising agricultural productivity by an infusion of capital to apply high-tech western practices that won't be sustainable. Will Bill Gates end up helping or hurting? Howard devotes much of his energy and money to working with villagers and experimenting with low-tech improvements such as no-till farming and using oxen vs.

tractors. The argument against fixing the world is: "What is right action with regard to the world?"

A primary, although not generally recognized, drive in human beings is truth-knowing. It starts with wanting to know the truth about the "external" world since we think it's the source of our suffering. Somewhere along the line we may progress to the view that we're not going to be able to bend the external world sufficiently to fix our problem, and we shift to an attempted manipulation of our internal world — i.e., changing our reaction patterns. All of these efforts really exhibit a procrastination of looking at the real source of the problem, which is not knowing the truth about what we are. The seeker moves from a focus on knowing the truth about the outside world to a focus on knowing the truth about the inside world, to knowing the truth about what he is. Knowing the truth about what we are is the highest ideal the human organism eventually conceives of. It no longer separates the knower from the known, no longer objectifies the object of suffering from the subject. To know the truth about what we are, we become Truth. Going within or becoming Truth may be the only way to gain a perspective that makes right action possible.

To get a trustworthy sense of what you really want, have you asked yourself what is your highest ideal?

❧

I tried getting more specific with things I'd want to change. I looked at specific things I've been teased about, at an embarrassing moment for my older brother that I remember, and at the fact of my younger brother's diabetes.

I noticed that the reason I might want to change the two things from my brothers' lives is if those things cause them emotional pain. In my own case, that's why I'd want to not be teased. It's not so much what I get teased for; it's the emotional pain that comes from it. I can see that I strongly believe that a big enough, strong enough emotion will totally overwhelm me and destroy that sense of me that I feel I am.

There's a vast difference between not wanting someone we care about (primarily ourselves, of course :-) to suffer pain and choosing to change a specific incident that has occurred if we had the power to do so. What might the repercussions have been if you had changed your brother's life so that he didn't experience that embarrassing moment?

Just as all longings can be traced back to the core longing, in my opinion, so can all fears be traced back to the fear of being overwhelmed. The organism learns to "handle" threatening situations like the Carnegie Mellon University robot vehicles learn to handle threatening terrain. Acceptance (in the Benoit definition) and emotions don't have any direct connection that I see.[5] Acceptance involves processing a vast array of data, which includes experiences and emotional reactions to experience, to distill the wisdom our computer is capable of computing relevant to the question of "Would I change it if I could?" The answer might come out as non-acceptance, but the process is not one of emotional reaction. This processing of massive data is what I'd call intuition. Sometimes—probably most often—the processing occurs "underground" and we only see the results. There have been a handful of times... one occurred recently... where I observed the operation in progress. The closest I could describe it would be like watching a database being read and displayed on a computer screen at the speed it's being processed. I awoke about 2:45 AM on

---

5   Hubert Benoit, in The Supreme Doctrine, distinguishes between acceptance and resignation. Unlike resignation, acceptance follows from considering something with our whole being and arriving at the view that we wouldn't change it even if we had the power to do so.

New Year's Day watching my mind doing that sort of thing...
only catching the highlights at a conceptual level... until the
job finished about 15 minutes later. The conclusion had an
emotional impact, but the processing itself was not at all like
an argument of fears and desires. The question that the mind
was trying to resolve was related to an emotionally painful
experience, but it was a question of trust, not of acceptance.
The process was, though, the same type of operation that I
witnessed when I had the "acceptance" experience in 1996.
I suspect what I've seen is what often goes on behind the
scenes preceding a "flash" of intuition.

*In writing about your realization, you mention: "[Harding] did his
tube experiment [...] with me as his partner, and I had a very clear
vision of what it was I was looking out from."*

*I tried this experiment several times and tried it this week with
a mirror. Is there anything else you can say about what you saw
you were looking out of that might be helpful?*

*I went through Harding's questions,[6] but still don't "get it."
My intuition clearly detects something of high value there, but my
intellect seems to override many of these questions. For instance,
my intellect jumps at the question "Could that face register as form
if you weren't void?" and quickly says "of course not, therefore
what's on this end must be a blank, featureless screen"(without
fully believing it) and thereby dismisses the question before any
actual seeing can take place. Any tips not involving lobotomy?*

I felt at the time, and don't have any reason to alter that
conclusion, that the new view from Harding's doing the tube
experiment with me was a result of suggestion. Some of us

6   http://www.headless.org/experiments/the-tube.htm

are more suggestible than others. For example, Shawn N. still doesn't get "feet being up" in his view! In order for the paradigm we're looking through to be replaced by a polar opposite, something has to either shock the mind or get it to temporarily suspend some belief. With a mentality that could easily argue three sides of any issue, I think that made me susceptible to the suggestion(s) implanted by Harding. You notice he doesn't simply say: "look into the tube… now what do you see?" It's loaded with suggestions, such as:

- Is your end closed, or open? (The correct answer is always the latter. :-)
- Are you face-to-face or face-to-no-face?
- Could that face register as form if you weren't void?

When you read the questions, don't proceed until you "see" (intuit)—not just lazily agree with or decide not to argue with—the view he's implying. Suspend the disbelief in the alternative view or paradigm.

What I recall having a very clear vision of was the conviction, when my "head" was in the alternative paradigm, that everything in the view was *inside* me. This was opposite to the conviction-view-paradigm I'd been operating in for the preceding 25 years, where anything in the view was *outside* me. My mind was convinced that both views were equally valid, which I found fascinating. What it did was to loosen up my convictions about "where" I was. Where do you believe yourself to be with respect to what you're viewing: inside or outside?

You mentioned in your update a desire to connect with your Source. That may not happen, or be apparent,

consciously. You probably remember my talking about how
I had a little vision one time about being connected with
something bigger than myself at the end of a long string. It
resolved the koan that had been with me for a day or two,
but there was no other apparent reaction. Several years later
I was watching the video footage of *Mr. Rose the Video*, where
he was talking with the Raleigh group who visited in 1991,
and I heard him say [which I didn't hear during their visit]
that we're still connected to our mind's umbilical cord...
and it clicked with me, then, that was exactly what I'd seen
in the vision. I don't recall ever "doing anything" about
it or "making use" of it, but I think it was another step in
the gradual loosening of my faulty self-definition. Others
occurred in dreams... and again I don't recall ever doing
anything with those or making use of them.

It's a natural unfolding, I believe, and maybe we can
accelerate it by somehow getting out of the way. The most
productive thing may be to focus on the biggest complaint
or koan the mind is aware of at the moment, coupled with
intuitive faith that knowing what we are may solve the
problem in an unimaginable way.

※

All I ever really wanted was to be close to my Source.

That's a beautiful articulation of what I believe to be
everyman's deepest desire. Since I happen to know that
you've never been anywhere but at your Source, it's easy for
me to see that there must be an under-scrutinized (faulty)
belief that tells you that you are separate from yourself. If
you give some consideration to what such a belief might be,
bringing it into the "light" may loosen its hypnotic hold.

✹

I have spent approximately 70% of my life as a negative victim with a large hole in my being... I have worked hard to change all that and within the last few years I have found love within and am more successful in living in the moment. Of course I continue to work my spiritual path, and know it is within and not without. Is being positive and the feeling of love the wrong direction; do I have to suffer to get to the question of I? And out of curiosity, where would you place me on the ladder?

It would be silly, wouldn't it, to court suffering. By my calculation, we're lucky if the happiness to unhappiness ratio in life is 10% to 90%. My feeling is to enjoy the happy periods and treat them as signs that things are going okay.

Suffering isn't necessarily related to unhappiness, though. Sometimes we suffer when we're happy and realize there's still dissatisfaction lurking in the background. I remember one time when I was living in Miami when I went through a period of weeks where every day I'd tell myself: "Wow, things are too good. They can't go on like this. Something bad must be about to happen." :-)

Have you considered joining the women's accountability/confrontation group? There are some good folks participating in it, and I've heard from a couple of skeptics who've seen that there's a great value in having others pepper us with questions and their differing conviction states.

There's a Canadian woman I don't think you've met yet... her name is H... who's been active in TAT for maybe 10 years. I remember my first presentation after my breakthrough in 2004 saying how everything depended on dissatisfaction. Afterward, H. said: "I'm not dissatisfied" and asked if that was a problem. She has also participated in most of the weeklong retreats we've held before the November

TAT meetings in recent years. And it wasn't long after 2004 that she realized she was deeply dissatisfied with her life. The word just had connotations she didn't want to associate with her idea of herself.

It's our deep level of dissatisfaction, of longing for X (wholeness, security, unconditional love, etc.) that propels us on the spiritual path... meaning the path to finding our true nature, of returning Home. When we get in conscious contact with that longing, that's the most productive part of making progress on the spiritual path, I feel.

I only have the vaguest memory of what's in *Solid Ground of Being*.[7] There are two more books I'm working on... have close to 300 pages of material in each so far but have more things to add and subtract. I heard from one fellow who said he spent more time with my book on his knee than reading it... which is exactly what I hoped would happen.

I don't find myself trying to place people on the ladder. My sorting seems to be more along the line of whether a person feels open (for questioning their beliefs) or not. You may be able to get an idea of where you are on the climb up Jacob's ladder from the "Three Questions" article in one of the old TAT Forum issues.[8]

❧

What is tension? Do you have a metaphor, analogy, experiment or activity I could try to know what it really is?

The word tension comes from Latin *tendere,* to stretch. Here are typical definitions of the term:

---

7   My first book, published in 2009 by TAT Foundation Press.
8   January 2007: http://tatfoundation.org/forum2007-01.htm#3

- The act or process of stretching something tight
- The condition of being so stretched
- The interplay of conflicting elements
- Mental, emotional or nervous strain
- Barely controlled hostility or a strained relationship between people
- Uneasy suspense
- A balanced relation between strongly opposing elements
- Voltage or potential

I had a recent inquiry from a mutual friend: "I never understood the thing about tension anyway. Maybe it is mostly for men?" My response: "You gave birth by Caesarian section? You don't have a mate?" And hers: "You are right—I like tension but do not let anyone know! :-)"

Life is tension. Life attempts to escape tension while being addicted to it. Look at your romance with nicotine, for example. Dead-serious commitment to knowing or becoming the truth parks us under the Bodhi tree.

❧

Re. your response to Paul ["I think it's tremendously valuable to see ourselves trotting out the same convictions of inadequacy, confusion, rationalizations, etc., time after time after time after…. And it's unlikely to register with us unless there's an audience. What keeps patterns from changing? Our machinery gets tired of the patterns and reacts with determination to change them. Since we don't direct our reaction-will, the explanation has to be something mysterious ('grace'). You've never been in a trap, in prison… you just haven't admitted to yourself that there's no wall behind you."]: *Do you mean that boredom with the incessant same old patterns playing out will finally lead us to admitting there's no wall behind us?*

It depends on your reaction to boredom. The generic reaction to boredom is, I think, to seek escape from the hound of heaven—i.e., distraction from the onslaught of truth.

❧

Intuition & Fears

I have a question about all this. This whole thing is looking confusing to me again. I have had so many insights and experiences, yet I still feel threatened when a client from work gets tense and irate around me. I would have thought that this would not be possible by now. All I can figure is that an unresolved childhood trauma is triggered or that I have not learned how to block other people's energy. I don't know much about energy but it seems I easily absorb it from others.

Two weeks ago, I saw clearly that what wakes up is not the body/ mind organism. It was very clear that there was only a story about an apparent someone on a progressive path towards something. I would have thought that this realization would have set me free. It does appear that since then I embody a present alert and aware state (for lack of better words) more consistently throughout the day. However, I do still get pulled out of this. Analytical work at my job and tense clients can trigger "separation."

So at this point I seem to live in this odd state where the lines between being here and not being here are blurred. Just like the lines between what is and is not possible seem to blur. Sometimes people look like real people and sometimes they look more like illusions or projections. And sometimes there is just me communicating and there are no assessments of who or what is or is not an individual.

So is this it? Have I lost my way somehow? I would have thought one of these perspectives would have become my "home" perspective. Instead, it keeps changing from moment to moment. There does seem to be a stillness that is consistently found. It is always there but maybe not as apparent at times. I feel an urge to take time off from the rat race to just rest into this stillness for a few months. I would also like this time to study more mystical topics and do some healing work on my body and mind. My intuition keeps telling me to do this, and I keep putting it off. What have other people done when this urge has arisen? It seems like a common move to make but my mind fights it as irresponsible.

Threats to our sense of self will continue to rock the boat until we know, by identity, what we are at our core. Even then the mind will still react, but there will be a background of knowing/identity that isn't rockable.

I'd say the body/mind organism is exactly what wakes up. What we are has never been asleep. Its body/mind manifestation has been cycling through various states of consciousness, which haven't included consciousness for you of what truly IS.

Your urge to take some time to rest in stillness is something to listen to. I wouldn't try to alloy it with other urges such as studying mystical topics and healing work. If you haven't done it previously, I think you'll find there are diminishing returns after a period of time. You might want to try it for a week then maybe a month.

I found that when I put first things first, everything else fell into place. It requires having faith, I guess. Richard Rose said that once a person makes a commitment to knowing the truth, he'd be protected. I found that to be accurate.

Intuition is a higher-level program or process of the mind… and much quieter than the umpire program that juggles the fear and desire voices. Our interpretation of intuition isn't perfect, so we have to check it with reason. The umpire process is basically oriented toward biological ends, and sometimes the intuition is going to point us toward something that could threaten our apparent security or comfort. The fear- and desire-egos or voices are primitive; the voice of intuition refined. We can put less importance in the former as we gain a broader perspective of the mind's operation.

I'm convinced from what I read that what's desirable from life is developing a soul. A rock of integrity and abiding nondual awareness. I think the most important thing is probably purity of intent. I personally have lots of doubt about my ability. I used to have lots of insights and have had some kenshos. But when I got into the moral aspect, I tried to be perfect and only be spiritual and got really judgmental of myself and others, and lost lots of clarity. Also I'm really confused about how much free will there is. I don't know how much I should resist the common life. I guess renunciation should primarily be an inner thing. It's OK to get married and so on but shouldn't be clung to as the end all be all.

Richard Rose used to say that the primary block to accomplishment that everyone faces is a conviction of their inability to achieve. When it comes to pole vaulting or calculus, we may have good data to show the probability or improbability of achieving success. But when it comes to finding the truth, there's no way to judge that. We don't have a clue. It really comes down to surrendering to or bowing to or admitting the implications of what we see. Renunciation may be pride's game. We strive to attain our highest ideal, which may become refined as we progress, and we achieve it through ultimate failure and the accompanying disillusionment that reveals Truth.

I am fully in-tune with the workings of the universe and the fact that nothing but Him exists. I can fully digest that I do not exist as an individual in a spiritual sense. This is at the logical and emotional levels.

I guess I am missing the experience. The experience of Nothingness and Everythingness.

I am half-way through your book, reading a couple of pages every day. I am totally in tune with what you are saying. I could have written your book, if my English was as good as yours!

My head is in it nearly all day. I am dissolving in something, and it is not life. It is more like death and I don't mind it. I am fully functional on the outside. But inside, I am like mud.

I guess I just don't know how to go forward from here. I have never had an out-of-body experience. But, I sense a guide (maybe an awareness) constantly with me.

When I study Rumi poems, they get deep into my mind/heart/ something else. Actually, when I read your writings, I have the same deep appreciation.

But, I feel as though I am in the mud. I do feel happy and sad normally. But, deep inside, I can't crack this. It is like a prison cell, tight and suffocating.

If there's still Him, then we're still hypnotized by the belief of being a separate something. There definitely is or at least appears to be a separate-something self... and the "no self" talk so popular in Advaita Vedanta circles these days is at best a half-truth. Have you seen the video of my talk at the Raleigh retreat last October?[9] I tried to show the opposite view... not that one is necessarily truer than the other, but if we see that two opposing views are equally valid/invalid, it may propel us to a higher viewpoint.

The idea of becoming "one with" Him (i.e., Other) also misses the boat. The only realization that takes us "to the other shore" is seeing/knowing/becoming/recognizing/etc. what we truly are.

---

9   SIG 2011 Retreat album, http://vimeo.com/album/1745120

Is the Sufi path a bhakti path, a path of intentional surrender?

Sorry to hear you agree with everything you're reading in the book. If it has any value, it's in seeing something that activates a response like: "Oh, I hadn't thought about that possibility." :-)

Unfortunately, we can't agree our way to Truth. (I tried that assiduously.) Truth comes by dislodging our beliefs, not strengthening them.

The conviction that we're "in" the mind, trapped in the mind, is part of the hypnosis. If you haven't yet read it, maybe the essay "The World Is Your Oyster"[10] on my website would give you an opposing view to chew on.

All Sufi paths are "surrendering to the will of God." Like all other ones, the two I have followed teach: God-in-the-center and nothing else. There is Nothing in the world (and other worlds) but God Himself. And He is Everything.

If your goal is to surrender to the will of God [which I hope you see is a concept referring to something you know nothing for sure about], then you need to discriminate between which actions (mental and physical) reflect your personal will and which ones reflect God's. This is the "doership" question, isn't it. How many of God's actions do you take credit for... in other words, pretending to be God?

There's got to be a simpler way to self-realization than intellectual and systematic arguments. How do the poor, uneducated seekers do it?

Could it be that I've already had it, but I don't know?

---

10   http://www.selfdiscoveryportal.com/arOysterWorld.htm

Do we do it, or does it get done to us? I think it externally affects us. I mean, He sends it when some conditions are met by us.

Does self-realization necessarily include the viewing of "Everythingness and Nothingness Simultaneously" experience?

The path is simple to the extent that we see through complexities. There appear to be two primary categories of seekers or their paths, one being the *bhakti* or surrender path of the feeling-type seeker and the other being the self-inquiry path of the thinking-type seeker. The thinker tries to find her self while the feeler tries to lose his self. I'm rather sure that all paths contain a mixture of both and that they converge to a point of simultaneously losing identification with the little self and "finding" the Real self.

You *are* it, but the body-mind you doesn't yet know it.

Part of the path is to see or discover the truth about doership... and then to continue to act in the face of paradox.

When you realize or recognize your true nature, what your "original face" looked like before your parents were born, you may then find the need to try to describe it in contradictory terms such as Everythingness and Nothingness.

Conscious Commitment

I've read that the #1 human fear is not of death but of public speaking. I can accept that as a possibility although I don't know what investigation led to it. Similarly, I don't know what the #2 human fear is. But if I were to guess, I'd say it's the fear of commitment.

We can look back at some project or period in our past and say to ourselves, "I was really committed... my actions showed how committed I was." Commitment is a key to successful accomplishment, but for some reason we don't always find ourselves committed to something we want to accomplish. We may find ourselves procrastinating the next step, which is often a step that would look trivial through someone else's eyes. We may start second-guessing our previous intention and the importance we placed on the objective. Something else may come along that gets our attention, and we forget what previously seemed important. We may look back in retrospect and be happy that we were diverted from pursuing the objective, or we may look back in regret, feeling that we missed an opportunity that may have changed the direction of our life.

If we regret a missed opportunity and find ourselves motivated once again to pursue the objective we abandoned, is there a way we can try to avoid a repeat failure? Consciously committing to accomplishing the objective may be a magical key to success. This is a whole different dynamic from attributing commitment to past actions. And it's not like making New Year's resolutions. Conscious commitment is looking and recognizing what we really want. First we have to get down below the noise of competing fears and desires to see or feel what we deeply want. Actually, I think we frequently feel it, but the mind may need to translate the feeling into some worded form to bring the feeling's message into fuller consciousness. Second, we need to scan our inner horizon to see or feel if we have any reservations. If we find significant reservations, then we aren't down to the level of recognizing our deep want. If we don't find reservations, then we can honestly say to ourselves that we commit to pursuing the objective regardless of what it takes.

It's our choice whether to be a cork on the ocean of life, carried in whatever way the currents of life may take us at any time, or to hoist a sail—to take advantage of favorable winds or to tack against unfavorable winds.

Walt Whitman—Camden, NJ 1891
Witness of the transient bliss of cosmic consciousness.

Scattering III

Confidence reduces insecurity when we intuit that something larger than our little-s self is taking care of things.

✿

Try not to take yourself too seriously. Self-deprecating humor may be an inverted form of seriousness.

✿

I-amness is a peculiar feeling that straddles the border between subject and object... like the Comanches in Arizona who raided back and forth across the Rio Grande, alternately hiding from the US Cavalry and the Mexican Federales.

✿

We notice what we're looking at in order to get our nose away from the painting. Eventually we get a more detached view of what we're experiencing. (Phase I.)

Where do we go from there? What can we really know about what we're experiencing? Nothing for sure. What's the only hope of knowing something for sure? Knowing the knower. (Phase II.)

✿

In the earlier stages of watching the mind, it often appears as if the mind has become more noisy. But it's just that we've become more conscious of the incessant activity. When we can hold two opposing views somewhat simultaneously, we reach an observation point that's anterior to them.

❧

Truly there's no more justification for hope than for hopelessness... but hope is more likely to produce action, both material (i.e., for the organism) and spiritual (for self-definition). The "right" kind of depression can give us a clearer perspective, but we have to climb out of the hidey-hole in order to act.

❧

Meditation = consciously watching what we're seeing. The goal of meditation = seeing the seer.

❧

Intuition eventually tells us—by interpreting the feeling of deep wanting, of the hole in the chest—that we want to return Home. But we've lost the way. As Rumi wrote, we find ourselves drunk in this tavern, not knowing how we got here; and therefore whoever brought us here will have to take us home.

❧

When we keep our primary fealty in mind, we don't have to try to mollify more than one lord.

❧

The formula for success has to include persistence. We persist until we see there's nothing in it for us... and then, not knowing why, we keep on.

❧

Do you want to *experience* unconditional love or to *become* unconditional love?

What if life *is* the experience of unconditional love? Do you find life self-satisfying?

❧

In this projected universe, we have a split between self and not self. Every thing in this dimension is *either* self or not self. We can look through a paradigm of not-self things being inside the self thing or a paradigm of not-self things being outside the self thing. So far, simple, right? Then we run into difficulty with the awareness thing. It has to be either a subject or an object, either a self thing or an object thing. But it seems to switch back and forth between being a subject and an object... sitting on the fence between both and neither.

❧

All our suffering can be traced back to a basic belief: that we are affected by what we experience. Maybe even prior to that is the belief that we are a thing. The mind can't conceive of a non-thing. The closest it can come is to imagine "empty space" around or between things.

❧

There's a limit to how much psychological stuff needs to be gotten out of the way. What seems to be most important is to get the core beliefs into view. These are mostly at a feeling level... but the feelings aren't the problem. It's the mind's interpretations of them that keep it from bowing to the truth.

❧

Jumping from one thing to another implies the pursuit of distraction. The pursuit of distraction implies something we don't want to face. We must either figure that it would be better to face it later or, who knows, it might not even be necessary if we can put it off long enough. But we'll never find Full Satisfaction while trying to avoid the truth tiger.

❧

Loving exalts the lover. Loving diminishes the lover.

❧

For the long-term stock market investor, a daily (weekly, monthly, annual) decline in the market isn't a failure. The path to Truth is a concatenation of dimishments.

Tunes III

When I was mentioning the people [I saw recently] in the nursing home and ego erosion, you pointed out that all of them had their egos eroded by time/age, but who is to say they gained anything by it?... Why don't those people (like those in the nursing home) whose ego has been eroded to shreds and body image destroyed, why are they not closer to the truth of who they are? I would have thought that challenge to self-image would bring one closer to who they really are. You had mentioned before... that life is a natural process of erosion of the ego, and I gathered that it was a valuable step. But what else do you think is needed, besides ego erosion and the suffering that comes along with it? What is it that those people are missing on their path to liberation?

I guess it depends on becoming conscious of the intuition, the nostalgia voice calling us home. Until that occurs, the machinery doesn't have any idea of where to feel in the dark. In other words, the vast majority of people don't seem to have been exposed to, or have heard, that there's a possibility of finding true Trueness. Many latch onto beliefs and use those as soporific mantras, as gentle lullabies. Others just sink into a conviction of impossibility and discouragement. How many people do you know whose philosophy of life is to just try to get through it with the least suffering, or optimizing the pleasure/pain ratio?

That's not to say that in the final breath their attention won't be drawn to its source. But wouldn't it be worlds better if it occurred 10 minutes or 10 years earlier....

❦

This week I felt that my friendships were everywhere rejected. I've been opening up since I sensed that I am ultimately unhurt no matter what others think of me. But lately it's been rough, as if I had forgotten how to feel safe. Now it feels like every time I offer love, I'm exposing myself to danger. And lately I've been feeling a lot of heartaches, even my forearms feel them too sometimes. I feel rejected, and I can't free myself from this feeling. And this in spite of me knowing that this is not true in all friendship cases. Why can't I turn away from this feeling of being unloved?

Emotions are a bitch, aren't they. Feeling rejected is one of the worst. It's not always an accurate interpretation, but knowing that doesn't diminish the feeling. An antidote is something like a reverse Harding exercise: switching from first-person to third-person view. (This doesn't even begin to happen until adolescence. I remember when my grandson Mark was a kid, he felt devastating rejection one time when I was merely teasing him by pretending I couldn't hear him through a glass-panel door.) Why would somebody "reject" us? Something threatens to overwhelm them. It's going to vary with people and vary at different times, but we're getting too close, they "need space," and so on.

When we talk about love, what do we mean? We want to be loved the way we want to be loved. It's a bit of a selfish endeavor, isn't it. And others have to play their roles the way we want them to in order to satisfy our requirements. Like "puppy love": we want to be loved unconditionally when we want attention and not to be bothered (by having to clean up after the puppy, listen to it cry at night, take it out for a walk when it's cold, raining, etc.) at other times.

❧

Hello, M. Here are some responses to your emails since my last one:

I am a slow learner and cannot objectively comprehend hard words of relative/subjective meaning like awareness and consciousness.

The important thing is to pick up a feeling of what the sentence or paragraph is trying to say. Richard Rose, for example, used words like those two interchangeably. It's important to have an idea of what each word in a sentence may refer to, but we can't get the importance of a deep sentence by guessing some "right" definition of each word. We can't understand our way to Truth. We feel our way, where *feel* and *intuit* are used interchangeably. By the way, false modesty is no more helpful than any other pretense.

I have been practicing (by intention) this "noticing" for some time now (say a couple of years; more steadily recently.) The challenge for me is to elongate the time that I notice myself performing an action like seeing, eating, thinking, etc. If I forget, then I somehow remember to notice myself performing again. Am I on the correct path to self-realization?

There is no correct path to self-realization. And the path isn't additive. There's no gradual increase in awareness that leads to self-awareness. That said, consciously noticing what we're seeing is "where it's at." But it's more a case of the depth of reaction than consciously riding the surface. Like pearl diving, maybe. Self-realization is the pearl beyond price that everyone's looking for, more or less consciously. We have to dive deep to find it.

Is self-realization a permanent state?

Self-realization is not a state of mind. After self-realization, the mind will operate in a relatively truer state than is possible otherwise.

I looked up doership, as you "defined." I like this word. However, all references I found were of Indian sources. Be it as it may. It serves the purpose. I am somewhat suspicious that the Big Guy (I mean God), independent of me is actually steering me. I say that because, again I have the suspicion that I am no-where to be found.

It might be instructive to read some of the books being put out by neuroscientists, such as David Eagleman's "Incognito," to provide some additional data on the doership/free will issue.

I don't know what makes this thing pop up from time to time. It does. It watches my normal states and conducts. It just watches. It surrounds me, and watches always from behind me. The me in this condition is the "busy body." The me is also very mindless and event driven. The me is trigger happy and is just running heedlessly.

Sounds like you're confusing subject and object in your *thinking about* what you're seeing. What...*you*... see.

The question is: What is our duty in life?

Who would we go to, to find out? If we follow an outside authority, we're trying to please or appease that authority in order to get what we want. A deeper layer of questioning, then, is to see what we really want.

❧

Do we have to reach a point where we loathe ourselves in order to become Love? As of now, I feel so consumed by my self-love. It just occurred to me that this love may be strongest when I feel most suffering. You're right, it feels like a fatal attraction. I sincerely believe that at the core of my sufferings and desires is myself. Yet I can't help but to love myself. Everything I do, I struggle for, is for myself. I am exhausted but I can't surrender myself. Is my situation hopeless?

No, dear friend, we don't have to loathe ourselves in order to become Love. We already are Love, and all we have to do is see through the illusory or delusory beliefs that obscure the truth. I think that journey typically goes through a stage where we see that there's not much difference between self (i.e., the individual we believe ourselves to be) and others... i.e., that our specialness is less impressive than our ordinariness.

Surrender is an experience, not something we do.

And don't be so impatient! (Actually, impatience is all right as long as we keep digging.) It takes time to gravitate away from befuddled states of mind.

❧

I've been reading and trying to answer the questions in your latest article[11] yesterday and today, and I seem to be stuck:

- You are what's observing. (True or false?)
- You are what's aware. (True or false?)
- You are what you're looking out from. (True or false?)

All intuitively true.

---

11   "Look at Awareness," in the February 2012 *TAT Forum* online.

- Where do all the objects (people, chairs, thoughts, feelings, and so on) that you're aware of appear?
- On a mental viewing screen?

I'm a bit confused about this. I have two versions: the default assumption I seem to operate under is that the external world is projected onto a screen inside my brain that I'm watching. Intellectual examination, or using the first person's point of view, makes this fall apart. From the first person's point of view, I can't distinguish between the external world and an internal screen. In fact, I only see the external world and its objects, but no screen. I can perhaps see that these objects have to be somewhere and that somewhere would be the screen, but that conclusion seems to only be an abstract intellectual construct rather than something that's intuitively obvious.

Any clues as to what I might be missing?

That's a good spot to keep looking and questioning.

When we see objects in the external world (quotes around we, see, objects, and external world :-) we don't see a screen behind them unless we're in a movie theater or have a really big TV screen we're sufficiently close to. They seem to be floating or moving in space or attached to something that's floating or moving in space. Light rays (waves? particles?) bounce off those objects and hit the rods and cones of our eyes, resulting in chemical and electrical changes, etc. But then we get to first-person experience, and then perhaps we have to construct metaphors to talk to ourselves or others about what/how we experience. We're pretty sure there's no physical screen on which the trees, thoughts, feelings, etc. that we experience appear. And we can only describe something by comparison. When it comes to seeing a tree, for example, do we experience it the same with our eyes open as with our eyes closed?

I forget where the line of questioning in the essay goes, but remember that any line of self-inquiry is eventually aimed at looking away from objects—from which we need to find temporary detachment. So my guess is that the essay is trying to work its way toward detachment from object-hypnosis.

✿

I became aware of my mistake in focusing on the "observed."

I turned my viewing "inside" and found the observer, who is me (I think). I cannot distinguish among the observer, observed, and the observation.

Interestingly, it is possible to observe myself with myself. This happens in a lockstep fashion and it has the side benefit of really absorbing me for minutes, maybe even longer.

I can see that self observing is a deep deep endeavour. I am looking for a door or a step-ladder to deepen my self-observation. It looks like a dark well.

How would you say I should dive deeper?

"How can I dive deeper?" is a prime candidate for contemplation, M.

Contemplation is a form of productive meditation... done by turning one's inner head away from what comes into the mind's view if it's not relevant to the topic or question. (You may recognize that as Richard Rose's prescription for meditation.)

Would you be interested in contemplating the question and reporting back on your observations?

✿

Art, I think I don't want to attain anything anymore. All I want is to die completely and absolutely. There is nothing in the world for me. I can't imagine anything I want. It doesn't even matter for me to know my Self or God, to be satisfied, to become this or that. I'm saying, there is nothing in it for [me], the only self that I'm conscious of. I don't want to survive. I'm still hanging around for my family. I would like to take a hike to Switzerland and then disappear. My little sister is 23, and we're close, and I love her. I don't have a heart to let her lose another family member at such a young age. But at the same time, my life as it is, is untenable. I cannot stop thinking about death. Maybe I'm overestimating my role in the family.

Here was my thinking when I found myself in the situation of seeing there was nothing in it (i.e., life) for Art:

- I admitted to myself that I didn't know what bodily death would bring... that it could be more of the same, better (e.g., eternal unconsciousness), or worse... and the probabilities were equal as far as I knew. We, or at least I, don't know how we got here this time, and I figured reincarnation is no more unlikely than incarnation. In other words, suicide might not solve the problem and could make things worse, not better.

- Having been around Rose, and later Harding, I felt that there was a possibility that one could indeed "die completely and absolutely" while alive... and I felt that working toward that was the best option.

I wasn't disappointed.

❧

What does it mean to hold up a mirror to oneself?

(I'll answer reluctantly, since it could be more helpful to leave it as a koan). It means turning the mind — the mirror — to the source of light.

❧

Because of Harding, perhaps, the source of the light seems it should be located in physical space roughly where my head ought to be (interestingly feeling a little back from the imaginary plane/window of observation). But if the light is awareness, it should have a source not pinpoint-able in 3D space, but transcending that somehow, like 3D in Flatland, lol, because 3D space is all observations/experiences.

So the image of holding a mirror to the source of awareness leads to trying to look at a spot, but I have sensed, somehow awareness should be outside space. So if I could ask a question I'd ask where is the source of light — where should attention aim?

It's an excellent question to ask oneself. Attention is the lighting up of an object in consciousness.

❧

I'm going to experiment with the no-control-of-moods thought. It doesn't seem valid in my experience. Beyond trigger avoidance. For example walking on the treadmill changes a mood. Controlling diet changes a mood. Moods exist and I don't control that, but it hasn't been my experience until most recently that I wasn't able to influence/control them. In Buddhism there is the concept of the seeds of moods, emotions and such, but mindfulness (breathing exercises, mere noticing walking) can meet and dissolve them. I believe I adopted a pseudo-conviction state (something not entirely believed but becomes a reactive pattern). 1. No control 2. Letting go of the desire to control the moods and such would lead to self-realization. If there was no control over moods CBT [cognitive behavior theory] would not work and it does in my experience and it's 89% effective in treating anxiety / depressive disorders. Do you have any thoughts regarding this?

The organism-us has varying degrees of reactive control over its reactions, as you say. I think people sometimes equate doership and control, but they're different issues in my book.

That's a very important distinction. Could you distinguish it for me?

Doership refers to the question of where's Waldo, the "doer" pulling the puppet strings or the creator of the automaton.

The automaton can be designed to react to varying inputs and control its reactions... like the robotic vehicles that the universities design to maneuver unfamiliar terrains. Some of its reactions could be electrochemical "thoughts" or "feelings" that might cause ongoing thoughts/feelings as well as physical reactions. If sufficiently sophisticated, it could "hear" its thoughts in order to react to them. It could have extremely sophisticated abilities to control its reactions. And some of those thoughts might be self-congratulatory ("look at what I did") or self-critical ("I really messed that up"). All the while, its creator could be monitoring its reactions. And its creator might be a more advanced automaton. :-)

❧

I am still being hit with weird happenings to the physical body. The vertigo is more or less gone unless I lay flat on my back and I will spin for a bit and then fine.

Latest was a couple of weeks ago. I had INTENSE panic, I would actually describe it as terror that came on while I was eating something, and it felt like my food would not go down. The intensity was full blown anxiety for about 2 weeks and is only subsiding now. Like running its course. Quite bizarre. I have lived on broths, and juices (good detox!) and have just been able to eat some cherries without going into panic that they would not go down. It is like a phobia. I have had something similar when I split up with my husband 10 years ago. But this time there is just no outward cause. A low-grade anxiety seems to run through my life all the time, but not to cause this.

Any thoughts?

You're having an "interesting" series of experiences related to your body, aren't you. When things like that happen to me, I generally ask myself first if the cause seems to be primarily physical or mental. For example, when vertigo hit me years back, there was an impression of a "psychic arrow" hitting me in the back of the neck that caused it. I don't remember having any theories at the time about where/why, and I still don't. The physical correlates seem to be some kind of middle ear thing according to medical science. Many events are doomed to remain mysteries. But I typically ask myself if there's some message in the event for me, and if so, what might it be.

With anxiety, my feeling is that it's like static affecting reception of signals. Not a feeling, exactly, and often obscuring the registration of feelings. Maybe that's its purpose. Anyway, I used to find that the only time my anxiety quieted and disappeared was during solitary retreats. And those times were generally when I was hit with inspirations, satoris, etc. I have a theory that when the mind relaxes, it's more likely to open. What it "sees" when it opens probably depends on what it currently believes about itself.

I find now that my mind sometimes anticipates events and even grieves for losses before they manifest. That reminds me of the dream I had one time in isolation, where Jesus visited me and told me: "Arthur, everything is going to be okay." Thirty days later, I think it was, my father died unexpectedly. Life, like a good novel or story, sometimes foreshadows events that are going to occur.

When we have a conscious life goal, we have a context for investigating and evaluating events that befall us.

❧

How could I have come from feeling so deeply appreciative and close from that first real correspondence from doing the exercise in your book? That feels like years ago and lots of miles but no real traction.

Feelings aren't necessarily an objective snapshot of where we stand, M. I remember after 20+ years I felt like I was back where I started—walking in circles in the dark with one foot nailed down. When I'd mentioned that to Shawn Nevins, who had preceded me down the path, he provided a different view.

Progress on the path to self-realization is through disillusionment. The illusions that prevent realization are the beliefs we have about what we are. The best record of milestones is keeping track of self-beliefs as they 1) are recognized consciously, 2) are subjected to doubt, 3) waver, and 4) are seen through. Interestingly, it's hard to get seekers to talk about their self-beliefs, much less chip away at them in a consistent fashion. I'm sure I didn't, either. We wait for life to provide conflicts, which eventually get us to question ourselves, and we may opt for creating intentional tension to try to speed up the process. Speaking of which, I forget if you've tried solitary retreats?

Looking back through my email archive, you'd written on April 9, 2010 that you were hoping that my book arrived from Amazon so that you could take it with you on a Caribbean vacation the next day. Apparently it did, as you wrote on 4/20:

> "I have to tell you I'm enjoying your book immensely. It is exactly the type of read I've been looking for. Despite a week in Aruba, (I read a lot on the beach) and both plane rides, I could not get through more than chapter 8 due to having to stop and actually run the work you suggest.
>
> "Right off the bat, I especially liked the One and the Same essay. Bang, right up against my head. I laughed out loud when I realized, yes, it is...it's aloneness."

If it inspired you, pumped you up, that's a first step. But disillusionment deflates us. The alternation between inflation and deflation moves us toward the truth of being.

❧

I have had some talks with a vicar that have been pretty interesting. We have discussed my relation with God or maybe my lack of relation. Not being confident that God is there for me.

Maybe there is reason to be fearful if I do not think God is there for me....

When you go there, you may find that there's nobody, no thing there. "God," unless it refers to some angelic or devilish deity, is in fact a pointer to what you truly are at the core of your being. God is not Other. The only relation between you and God is one of identity. You're speculating about some concept that's been passed along and mutated until it no longer resembles what the concept points at.

✿

Is it true that a good life is an engaged life? The kind of inspired engagement I experience when writing my work is precious moments for me. The good kind of losing myself into something more precious than myself. But the hectic kind of being lost in daily activities, I don't value as much since I feel I miss what happens even when I experience it.

I'd say that a good life is one that functions according to the person's "highest light." We don't know what the purpose of a flower bud is until or unless we see what impact it has on its surroundings. One bud's purpose may be to inspire a thought or action on the part of a viewer. Another bud's purpose may be to burst into a bloom whose scent attracts a bee to spread its pollen. Another's may be to produce a seed that keeps that species going. From the bud's standpoint, if it's a conscious-of-self bud, I'd say a good life is one where the bud pursues its deepest/highest desire or blueprint. I think that happens when we see-or-feel (intuit) what we really want, and our lower-level feelings don't prevent our acting on it. We learn to act in the face of fear, but with discernment.

✿

Regarding the following excerpt from a talk by Richard Rose,"Definition of Zen,"at Kent State U, circa 1973:

> Now this is what they really mean in this Zen literature about no-mind. They mean the point where the head stops. And they talk occasionally about killing the Buddha, or killing the mind. But you can't kill your mind. These were terms that were either lost or had something wrong with the translation, or misinterpreted. The mind

is killed for you. You can't set out to kill your own mind. The only thing you can do is set out to find the truth. But in the process of finding the truth, you have to somehow put a stop to this relative hassle that goes back and forth: "It could be this but it also could be the opposite. Or let's look at it from two sides." No, you have to go right down the middle. Look at it directly. Become one with it. You can't reason it out, back and forth.

Is the middle just plainly seeing what you're looking out of and at? Like Harding's bidirectional attention without intention?

I don't know if Harding would have agreed, but based on my observation of the mind, the bidirectionality of two-way seeing is like an alternating current... attention is either directed outward or backward at any instant, but not both.

Looking outward, we see the truth of a percept, such as the picture of a tree that appears in our mind, merely by noticing the percept. If the thought "oak tree" is triggered by the percept, we may have to do some investigation to determine the truth of that concept.

When we feel the sense of self, our I-amness, we look backward, in the direction of what/where we're looking out from, to see or find it. And typically we don't see or find anything when we look back in that direction. In fact, what we're looking for seems to jump behind us quicker than our attention can find it.

But at some point, most always after years or decades of struggle, we become conscious of awareness. By that I mean that we can somehow see or look directly at awareness. We don't see any thing, but if we look sufficiently, we become consciously aware of its singular characteristic. Once that occurs, if we've previously whittled our individual self-definition down to the last faulty remnant, that last remnant will be exposed as an illusion. At that point, the observer merges with the observed. We recognize the Truth by becoming it... or become It by recognition.

❧

Response to a previous comment ["It appears you're looking for music that enhances your sad mood. Life is not all sad (or all cheery)]: *if life is not all sad, not all cheery, then what is it?*

Life is the struggle to become what we are.

[*And:* "The spiritual quest requires steady persistence... and that requires persistent dissatisfaction... a BIG problem the mind can't escape"]: *Maybe surprisingly, the way I look at my life experiences generally is with a sense of them being special or, yes, maybe blessed. I feel the difficult experiences are the ones more valuable because of the people I met during these. It's especially the friends I made, like you, that made me feel blessed. Yet it doesn't make me stop feeling I'm constantly writhing in pain. Yes, that BIG problem is sooo uncomfortable, to use a euphemism. And there's a sense of exhaustion (and maybe also resignation) that made me long for complete death.*

The BIG problem is resolved by going "in, down and through" it, not escaping "up and away" from it (phrases used by Douglas Harding to describe the journey through existential pain).

❧

I can feel that I am nothing when I look back, nothing and everything. Awareness pure and simple. No thought, no mind, no judgment, no bias. No wanting things to be other than what they are, no wanting at all. Is there a witness there or not? I don't get the feeling of the witness, not like I used to.

Feelings (I am nothing, nothing and everything, etc.) are "there"—i.e., objects of consciousness. "No thought, no mind, no wanting" etc., are concepts... also over there. If there were a witness "there" it would have to be "other" (someone else, something else). Jesus apparently told his disciples, who asked him to take them with him, "Where I'm going, you cannot come." You cannot see what you're looking for from "out here." You have to come "in," where you—the "you" identified with beliefs about what you are—cannot go. The "you" you believe yourself to be cannot see the witness that you are.

The best I can describe the feeling [my longing] is something like "embrace." I think of my younger years, when there would be a distinct feeling—usually when I was with family—that arose, a sort of "coziness." The feeling had something like "comfort" associated with it. A feeling of "security," like nothing could hurt me in that space. Not necessarily happiness, though I was often happy, but more of a beingness. I could just sit there in that space, with many people (extended family) around me, and feel satisfied. No need to move or speak. I've started to feel a similar thing after Quaker meetings lately; I'll just sit there while everyone gets up and converses. Someone usually comes over and then I figure I'd better get up and converse—they may think I'm being anti-social.

I had a similar feeling on the bus ride to school in high school. It was just a 15 minute trip, but sometimes about two-thirds of the way—I'd find myself in this trance—just staring out the window—I didn't want it to end (it might have had something to do with the gas fumes, or road vibrations?). Anyhow, that's the feeling. Nothingness, comfort, coziness, security, embrace.

"Nothingness, comfort, coziness, security, embrace"—
The complexion of your original face—
"The one Meaning giving worth to all effort....
"Closer than home, country or race"[12]—
We put in the effort... the rest is all Grace.

> "That's one side of the equation—persistence. The one you have control over. The other side is grace. A person on the path has help. Once a person makes a commitment to the Truth—I mean truly demonstrates a sincere desire to find his Real Self at all cost—then this commitment will attract assistance and protection. Opportunities arise. Blocks are removed. Decisions may even be made for you." —Richard Rose, *Zen and Common Sense* talk

✄

Having some Gestalt-like moment of ah-has. It has to do with other people and strangers mostly. I have a feeling it's nothing other than learning to be more empathetic towards others. Any ideas why this could be occurring towards strangers and not people so much people directly in my life?

Waking experience is similar to dream experience in many ways. In dreamland, our inner dream-maker communicates with us in varying ways to get our attention and to "wisdom" us. One of Richard Rose's understated gems is that "definition requires comparison." Self-definition is a provocative

---

12   From the poem "Nirvana" in Franklin Merrell-Wolff's *Pathways Through to Space."*

wording for self-realization or self-recognition. To recognize the Real Self, we need to lose our identification with a limited self. Losing that identification requires a graying of the line between self and other. We're more inclined to help a relative or friend—closer association with our limited-self identity—than a stranger. Less personal is more universal.

🌿

Have any ideas as to inquiry meditations moving forward? Have any ideas as to any type of meditation moving forward? I think I hit the end of the road with that last one. Going after my "I" is like backing away from my finger now. The hub of the wheel is gone—the one I was aware of. Any questions pop into your head that I can ask? I tried to inquire as to the ownership feeling of thought and it's not believed now, so it's not compelling me to inquire. I can't see how it's not me thinking as I can't see how it's not me seeing, hearing, tasting, it's just the objects of seeing hearing tasting and such are not separate from the seeing, hearing, tasting. (At least it doesn't seem that way.) I do find that I'm thinking about "myself" with equal frequency. It's just that it's focused on trying to figure out what is going on, but it doesn't have a point to explore... for example, the above with the feeling of ownership over thought....

The conviction of being stuck in this oyster world, playing out a death penalty, results from being identified with what we're experiencing.

There wouldn't be any light in the oyster if it didn't have an opening.

The opening is the light of awareness, which includes the feeling of I-amness.

Looking back in the direction of I-amness, we see "nothing" (i.e., the dazzling-darkness aspect of Light).

We have to back into the awareness until the moment of turning around occurs… when the vector reverses, in Richard Rose's language.

Backing into awareness involves backing away from faulty beliefs about what we are. If we conclude we are nothing, or that there's no separation between what we are and what we experience, etc., we're stuck. If we admit we don't know what we are but persist in trying to find or define the elusive self, then we can move. The seer changes or evolves from being mired in the swamp of emotions to the umpire or decision-making view, then to the process-observing view. From there, the miracle of individual consciousness of awareness coincides with a reversal of the seeking vector.

❧

I'm aware of this resentment I carry, but a long time ago, I decided that it wasn't productive at all to the search, and have ever since usually looked away from it. I don't even know what entity to direct the resentment at, which makes it worse. I know pop psychology holds that repression of negative feelings is not good, but in this case, I don't see an alternative.

Feelings are data. Once they're felt they become part of intuition's database. When they generate ongoing left-hemisphere drama—woven into the story of the imagined self—that provides additional data for intuition's processing. We are that which watches/awares. All mental activity is reaction. That which we observe is cosmic machinery.

❧

I feel I'm more identified than ever with every thought that happens to get shot into my personal awareness.

This sounds like it has a tinge of panic to it, J. As with V., I wonder if there's a conviction behind your negative emotions that is producing the physical ailments you've been experiencing. Any recurring pattern of negative experience may be trying to focus our attention on something we don't want to look at. Repression may have unwanted consequences. Perhaps relaxation—i.e., relaxed contemplation—would bring additional clarity.

By the way, I just remembered that one of my pre-awakening periods of most intense clarity was when my body was hanging on the edge of vertigo for several hours... hugging the toilet on my knees and subject to intense nausea if I so much as moved my head a bit off center.

Moundsville, WV, USA

Considerations for Any Life

Are you here, alive, for a purpose?
If you believe you are, or if you believe you're not — how do you know for sure? Would an honest position be to admit you don't know for sure? And if that's the case, do you want to know if it's possible to know something for sure?

Do you want to live a life aimed at finding a big-picture view of what your life is all about? Are you that which is experiencing, that which is aware? Is there a way to inquire inwardly as well as outwardly? Can anything be known for sure until the knower is known?

If you're dedicated to knowing the truth about your life, can you find it by looking, or do you have to "go there"? Would the finder remain separate from the found or "become" it? What is your true identity?

To find the truth of self, would you strive to live life truthfully? To strive productively, would you establish a plan and work at it regularly? Is it something you can do on your own, or would it be better to find others to work with?

Live... inquire... know.

Look within... go within... become.

Seedlings IV

Dead-serious commitment parks us under the Bodhi tree.

※

I'd received an inquiry from a guy saying he was trying to expand the number of moments when he was consciously aware and wondered if he was on the right path. I was formulating a response about how self-realization isn't additive or progressive in that sense, and what's necessary is one deep dive. It occurred to me that there may be an analogy with pearl diving… that no matter how long we swim on the surface, we have to dive deep if we want to find a pearl. Of course the analogy breaks down in that we can't take a deep breath and do the dive intentionally. Seemingly it happens by accident when things beyond our control line up just right. Our life-actions may be like a prayer that eventually causes that alignment.

※

The mind is a problem-solving machine, and it focuses on the problem which has its immediate attention. The only time it gets around to the "big" problem is when the more immediate problems are taking a momentary break. The way we encourage that activity, I think, is by carving out time for it.

※

The mind is a probability-weighing machine, endlessly calculating and recalculating the best path to take—like a GPS navigation computer. The maps and software are continually updated by our life experience.

❧

Intellectual processing is necessary to balance the feeling side of the mind, but the intellect can process life-experience and come up with different conclusions based on the mood of the moment. The intuition's processing takes mood and other factors into consideration, but it only changes its conclusions as life-experience accumulates.

❧

Confrontational questioning in the context of self-inquiry is not supportive. Its purpose is to rock the boat, not the cradle. That doesn't mean it has to be an overt attack. The best confrontation, usually accidental, comes in from the side. Its value is in getting us to take a fresh look at a belief, which undermines our sleepy delusions.

❧

In some way we have to get a high enough perspective to become unmoved by mind-movement (or mind-movement stops for us) and then sink deep for the pearl beyond price.

❧

When the mind is finally able to look steadily at awareness, it will see (intuit) what has prevented it from seeing the Truth of Self.

❧

Hope is, or can be, painful… but we generally can't act unless we follow a ray of hope.

❧

My "formula" for the seeker: 1) carve time out of your schedule daily to remember/feel what you want and then notice what you're seeing, and 2) carve longer periods of time out of your schedule occasionally to go off by yourself, away from distractions, with time to do the above and time to do nothing. The pregnant periods for going within are periods where there's nothing to do following reasonable exertion/struggle to go within.

❧

Attention: What we see when we notice what the light of awareness is shining on at the moment. Noticing is paying attention.

❧

We're born alone, and die alone. We come from The Alone and return to The Alone… and not just at birth and death.

❧

There's a mentality that leans strongly in favor of avoiding planning and an opposing mentality that leans strongly in the other direction. Both dispositions are based on strong convictions about self (and other)… the very things that keep us bound in ignorance of Self. So the "prescription" to cure the maladies might be to intentionally act contra-ego… i.e., for the convinced non-planners to challenge their belief-state by intentionally planned action and for the convinced planners to challenge their belief-state by intentionally unplanned action… while "scientifically" observing the experiment.

＊

Sex centered in the head, which seems to be the default male pattern, is very limiting. One of the brilliant and under-appreciated pearls of Richard Rose's teachings is that definition requires comparison. The mind only knows something in terms of its opposite. We can only enjoy to the extent that we've suffered, for example. To get a perspective on how the mind "uses" eating, we need some experience of fasting. Intentional fasting is preferable to imposed fasting, I'd argue. To get a perspective on how the mind uses sex, we need some experience of intentional chastity.

＊

When we're driving on snow or sand and the car wheels are spinning but the car's not moving, if we goose the gas, we may just get ourselves into a worse condition. Sometimes we can ease our way out by gently rocking the car forward and backward.

Melodies IV

Do you think the end of suffering is the start of life? Or do you think life can be fully lived even while suffering?

I'd say that the life of the new "unit of suffering" starts at conception but that existential suffering begins when we become self-conscious a few years after birth. Self-consciousness brings on the fear of annihilation based on the conviction that "I'm an individual something that can be hurt." The end of existential suffering comes when we know what we truly are at the core of our being.

Living life fully means consciously pursuing self-inquiry for the purpose of self-definition. Self-knowing occurs simultaneously with the death of self-delusion. All definition requires comparison. Life can only be seen in contrast to its opposite. Knowing what you are brings a radically new perspective to life.

¥

If the mind really is just a dead end, like an unchangeable wall in front of me, what does that really mean? Is there a way out? All the ways lead back to that wall and in some way strengthening it.

The mind is the dimension of conscious experience. It has no walls or other boundaries. The feeling of being trapped in the mind is based on faulty (delusory) beliefs about the self. I tried to convey a contradictory view in an essay titled "The World Is Your Oyster."[13]

---

13   www.selfdiscoveryportal.com/arOysterWorld.htm

I don't feel that I am capable of any intense effort at this point. Do you think this is a bad thing? Or is there value in "gently pushing"?

I think all efforts are responses to how deeply we feel our dissatisfaction. Notice the theme for the June TAT meeting:[14] "Your House Is Burning: Urgency on the Spiritual Path."

❧

What are some questions to ask oneself to check for sincerity/or lack thereof in this process? I am beginning to feel more 'alone' after an intentional consolidation of group involvement/input from many to a few guides. A transition is occurring from being more vocal with others, to limiting discussion to fewer people. A more private process. A lot of doubt is arising from this; yet something seems to be sincere and continuing to move forward. Yet what this something is, is indefinable. Any feedback on this process that I am describing might be helpful.

I think the way we check for sincerity is to notice the motivations for our actions. That may be in response to an underlying question of why we acted as we did. When actions are determined by a contest among our fears and desires, we see that most actions are based on which "team" makes the most noise. The quality of our decisions goes up as the voice of silence (i.e., intuition) affects the decision-making program. But we need to discern whims from higher intuition.

You seem to have many irons in the fire, J. Perhaps that's the result of your feeling alone. Simplification is part of the nostalgia or longing that's pulling us Home, and that may be something you're acting on. I had the feeling that I needed

---

14   www.tatfoundation.org/june/tat_june_gathering_2012.htm

to learn to "think for myself," as you also mentioned. I feel that's an important pull... but potentially misleading. Here's a short item I wrote in *Solid Ground of Being* titled "Strategy for Knowing the Self":

> The strategy for self-definition requires *becoming your own authority.* How is that done? By doing it on your own? By not being influenced by others? I've known people who have followed those strategies, and I agree that they are effective—for isolating yourself from possibly useful influences. They're really two sides of the same coin, the former ("no help") motivated by pride and the latter ("no influence") by fear.
>
> It's far better to immerse yourself with people who are striving for what you're striving for, including those who may have preceded you down the path. But carve out alone time for yourself—daily, and occasionally for longer periods.
>
> Do you become your own authority by thinking for yourself? I used to feel that it was the solution, but when I saw that all thinking is a reaction process, I realized that thinking for myself was literally impossible. What is possible, though, is to *look* for yourself with an unbiased eye not affected by thinking or feeling.
>
> Whatever set of fears and desires is making the most noise determines your action or inaction—until there's sufficient detachment from identifying with the view (i.e., those fears and desires). To look objectively means not flinching from the contradictions you'll see about what you believe yourself to be.
>
> Our primary desire is for *eternal survival in a state of grand equanimity.* We arrive at that state when we realize the truth that "God loves us." The purest form of love is identity. God is all; all is God. Thus the search for permanent satisfaction is the quest for knowing the self, for self-definition.

❧

A friend quoted something that Shawn Nevins had written[15] ["Mr. Rose told me that everyone has a different obstacle and unless they opened up to him, he couldn't help."] and asked: What obstacles do you see in me? Have I opened up enough?

He was trying to encourage Shawn, who was a closed book in some ways, to open up to him. He eventually told Shawn that he had his heart in a closed or locked box. (That puts his early remark to Shawn, "You can also feel. Maybe you'll use both. I don't know," in perspective, doesn't it.)

The teacher listens to words and, more importantly, to what *isn't* said. The obstacles take the form of, or rest on, feeling-level beliefs. The male mentality generally wants to go into a cave and wait for his feeling-level problems to go away. But to get perspective, our feeling-level beliefs need to come under the light of conscious scrutiny. Our feeling-level beliefs about what we are come into view and are then seen as being shaky. The solution to existential suffering is to know what we are, which occurs when we die while living.

Help comes in the form of encouraging us to look at our beliefs. In the early stages of the search, that may include pointing out some of the beliefs. But in later stages, pointing them out directly isn't likely to help. The question for the seeker working with a teacher he trusts to ask himself is: "Have I opened up enough?"

❧

---

15   Quotes and Notes: Meetings with Richard Rose, 1991-1996, in the August 2005 TAT Forum *www.tatfoundation.org/forum2005-08.htm*

Last week I went to visit Sailor Bob [Anderson] again. Craving being near someone physically who has woken up. He is very Advaita speak, so much of what is suggested is just that. It feels though when he points to what you really are being that sense of presence that you are aware. Is that it? When there is no thought or between thoughts there is silence and a sense of being. Is that True Nature? That nothing?

The sense of presence, of being what's aware, the feeling of I-amness, silence... those are like readings the mind gets of our true nature. Those are experiences of the mind... and the doorway back to our essence. Going back through that doorway, we discover our true identity... and from "back there," we view the mind-dimension with its perceptions and projections.

❦

Whenever I've been able to set goals or follow some course of action I always end up giving up because of those feelings of being incapable of doing anything....

When we "hear" a thought, where has it come from? (I remember the first time I did a solitary isolation, the "Mary Had a Little Lamb" song would run through my head and I'd think WTF!) They come out of "nowhere"—we know not where—and return to nowhere. As far as we know, there's some invisible stranger whispering them into our awareness. If they're familiar, we conclude: Oh, that's just me talking to myself. If they're unfamiliar, we think: Where did that come from??

You've become thoroughly familiar with thoughts of "being inadequate, not good enough, and incapable in general." Thus you believe them, as if they're from an authoritative source. (Who or what invisible source is the authority?) Once ingrained, the mind adopts those beliefs as accurate descriptions of an unknown "self" that's responsible for the thoughts and actions that we witness this body "doing" or having. If we're convinced it's not possible to question the unseen authority, then we're seemingly stuck. And the ropes are pulled tighter if we give the authority for our lives over to other people. The mind looks for evidence that supports its beliefs, as miserable as those beliefs make us. We look into the eyes of everybody around us, project our self-beliefs into their territory, and then read the self-condemnation (that we project) in their eyes.

His bottom line seems to be that you should entertain the possibility that there is no you… He seems to continually try to get his audience to look at how the self is constructed and how unreal it is.

The idea of looking to see that something doesn't exist makes absolutely no sense to me. The primary data of our existence is a feeling of I-amness. (Isn't that the source of all our suffering?) Discovering what we truly are holds out the only hope for relief. (And yes, it may very well reveal that what we currently believe ourselves to be isn't true.) We—these body-minds—are arguably here so that our real self can "know" itself. Our existential discomfort is the thorn in the side that causes these organisms to look for relief. And Total Relief comes when the organism succeeds in that mission. The organism-us has two options: act or not. Act in the face of great uncertainty in order to find Certainty, or try to hide.

※

I have been troubled a lot recently by thoughts and feelings of [the specifics aren't important] and related regrets. This is one area that seems irresolvable and keeps me locked in depression and hopelessness.

A conviction state (like depression/hopelessness, for example) selects material that reinforces it.

❧

Richard Rose suggested that a person could sit in rapport with themselves.[16] *Tried this briefly one morning, and it seemed to have a different feel even though I had no idea how to go about it. Maybe it was only the power of suggestion. How does one go about it? Does one have to set the table so to speak for a favorable condition, as in feeling true friendship with oneself, or is it a matter of simply tuning in to a silent presence within?*

I'm no authority on rapport... but it sounds to me like your question may be a perfect koan for you. It also brings to mind the account I remember reading about how during the Civil War, troops shooting at each other would call a temporary peace... exchange tobacco, chat in a friendly manner... then resume the battle.

❧

I googled the phrase "egoless vector" and that took me to your article called "Magnetoresistance & the Search for Self."[17] *It is incredible how much that article tracks the evolution of the question "What*

---

16   5/15/94 - Rose did say that a person should sit for rapport with themselves. This was different from meditation because the mind would eventually go blank in meditation and it'd turn into dreaming. ("Quotes and Notes: Meetings with Richard Rose, 1991-1996" by Shawn Nevins; http://tatfoundation.org/forum2005-08.htm#15)

17   www.selfdiscoveryportal.com/arMagnetoresistance.htm

am I?" in "my" mind. Within the last six months I have definitely moved from the phase of "I see it as the only hope" to the phase of "hopelessness." It has become blatantly obvious there is nothing in this search for "me" and in fact the "ego-sense" trying in any way with any practice to erode the "ego-sense" seems like nothing more than more ego sense trying to fulfill another desire. Hence, a steady feeling of hopelessness and even dread when I think about the search and the practice. And yet, and maybe it is this egoless vector Rose spoke of, I absolutely can't stop searching and searching. I burn through book after book, meditate religiously, all the while knowing if something is going to wake up it isn't going to be me, rather whatever wakes up has to wake up from the sense of "me" and that seems like something "I" have absolutely no control over.

Continuing to work despite a feeling of hopelessness is a good sign. Setting up time at the end of work periods to do nothing can create the opportunity for a dynamic opening. Have you tried a solitary retreat?

❧

Referring to the December 1, 1993 entry from Shawn Nevins's journal[18] ["Talked to Mr. Rose. I asked why I didn't pick up on things like others. He said he thought I was sensitive, but my sensitivity was in a locked box. He said I was reserved. He said that's fine, you can just be that way, and let others do the talking. I said don't I have to change if I want what you have? He said yes and that's what you work on in meditation."]: What do you work on in meditation? How should I meditate?

---

18   "Quotes and Notes: Meetings with Richard Rose, 1991-1996" by Shawn Nevins; http://tatfoundation.org/forum2005-08.htm#15)

Productive action requires an objective, a plan, and working with others. We don't accomplish anything significant without help from others and helping others.

The issue of meditation isn't a technique... it's about a struggle to free oneself from a restricted state of being.

You can work on changing... sometimes a change in "scenery" (like trading up addictions, e.g.)... with the objective of making yourself accident prone for getting to a more interior viewing position and then, eventually, the grand accident of discovering your true identity.

❧

The backing away [from untruth][19] sounds very simple but when I try to apply it, I run into trouble. How do I do this? For example the promise of satisfaction by a sexual action is a lie. I've found out a zillion times. And yet the turning away of my attention is not good enough as the intensity of the action gets so high that my functioning in the world gets jeopardized. And trying to function in life while being absent minded and empty because of the inner battle raging is also a distraction for any serious practice. So how do I back away from untruth in this situation? Art, do you have any idea that might be helpful here? I've looked into this question another zillion times; I know exactly what happens and how, but the continuous struggle makes me wonder every time if there is something I might have missed. It beats me what it could be though.

Suppose I'm a tobacco user, I've been exposed to the arguments for why tobacco use is harmful, I now believe that tobacco use is harmful, and I want to stop. But despite my

---

19   3/3/92— Rose, "You don't fight battles by worrying about what you may lose." "You'll never know if what you're doing is right. You can only back away from untruth." From "Quotes and Notes: Meetings with Richard Rose, 1991-1996" by Shawn Nevins (op. cit.)

efforts, I haven't been able to stop successfully. My "issue" wouldn't be confusion about backing away from untruth. It would be: "Why hasn't knowing the truth about tobacco use set me free from my addiction?"

We back away from untruth when a belief hits the wall of disillusionment. The belief that keeps the tobacco addiction in place is probably below my level of conscious recognition. But if I watched/listened closely to the argument that preceded the lighting of the next cigarette, or insertion of the next plug of tobacco inside my cheek, I would see the belief that wins the argument (e.g., "I've gotta have this or I'll get agitated") and the belief that prevents an executive veto of the action (e.g., "I deserve this," or "I'm too weak to resist"). Those are beliefs about the self that may be illusory.

Any addiction may give us all the data we need for self-realization.

※

The fellow who introduced me to the [Greg] Goode experiments sent me a link this morning to a video of an interview with Rupert Spira who does as good a job as anybody these days of describing the nondual view in common-sense terms.[20]

A potential problem I see, A., is like what Richard Rose described about Bucke's *Cosmic Consciousness* collection: It included examples of two groups of testimony, which Bucke wasn't able to discriminate. Listening to the first two minutes of the Spira interview, where he defines nonduality, my impression is that he's talking about the unitive view — like Whitman's, for example, or Jill Bolte Taylor's. It may be a reflection of the mind's seeing the "everythingness" aspect of identity.

---

20   https://non-duality.rupertspira.com/watch/interview-with-lilou-mace

Spira's further discourse is not as superficial as the typical no-self conclusion that the neo-advaitins often talk about. But at about 20 minutes into the interview, he says:

> Thought divides hearing into two parts: the self on the inside that hears and the sound on the outside that's heard. That's duality. But if we stay close to our experience... hearing is not divided into two, a me part and a not-me part... it's just hearing, one intimate substance... And seeing is the same... you invade the entire field of your experience; nothing is separate from you...

For someone like Spira, Whitman, or Taylor, I presume they're accurately describing the view they're experiencing. It's more appealing than the "normal" human view and therefore appeals to the mind searching for absolute X. Spira's description of the search for love or completeness (around minute 25) describes the seeking for X nicely. Some of us may experience our everythingness first before the final recognition, and it could be a very pleasant vacation. But this type of seeing that we're not separate from what we're seeing *may* not (will not, in Art's opinion :-) expand our identity beyond individual consciousness and its dependence on a body. How could it?

❧

What have you found to be an effective tool for opening up the emotional center?

I had never tried intentionally until about a year and a half ago. I found it by consciously letting down all my defenses with another person. I found recently (while driving by myself at the beginning of an all-day drive) that the same technique worked to get below the "arguing voices" to feel very clearly what I wanted regarding a close personal relationship. I think of it as "getting down to love."

※

Regarding the process observer: how closely are/were you able to witness the workings of your mind? Is this done at actual time, or upon reflection?

I've been able to witness a good deal of the mind activities directly, but at the process observation level (above the level of directly witnessing percepts, thoughts and feelings as they move across the viewing screen) witnessing operations like decision-making and intuitional computation in slow motion has happened only on rare occasions and held me "stopped in my tracks." I have the feeling that it leaves the neural system unable to instigate voluntary (as opposed to autonomic) activity.

All you have to do is witness one of these operations once in order to see that you're not "doing" it. And I don't think it's necessary to see them directly. It's like a jury trial… all that the mind needs is sufficient evidence to convince it one way or the other (about "doing" in this case). The jury, if wise, knows that it can never know anything with absolute certainty. The *jnani* knows that nothing can be known for sure other than the knower.

※

I've been struggling with drinking on the weekends but have been keeping up with my journal and meditating during the week. Quitting drinking cold turkey seems like a hard one for me right now so I'm trying an experiment with curtailing my drinking habits...

It's good to experiment with what works effectively for us in accomplishing objectives. For my mentality, cold turkey was easier than moderation or gradually easing out of things. It's just a question of trial-and-error and finding out more about how our "machinery" works. Life is truly a schoolhouse for M. and Art... but underneath it all, it's how Awareness self-awares. Maybe it would be more neutral to say how It self-its, or better yet, how Isness ises. :-)

❧

Just noticed something while riding my bicycle, had a thought about the wonderful freedom of nature which elicited an almost immediate feeling of longing in my heart. Then I thought that fear feeling in my body is similar to feeling the longing in my body... stomach/ heart chakra area. The difference is in intensity/interpretation. I can get away from/dissolve the fear one and the longing one doesn't go away. Can this noticing be helpful to me, or is this a dead end too?

I think that feeling the longing is the best incentive for finding what answers it. Just feeling it for a few seconds before starting meditation or self-inquiry reminds us of our biggest want. We don't know how to find IT, which confounds and sobers the mind. Yet despite the seeming impossibility, we persist... and magic is right around the corner, waiting.

❧

The deepest desire thingy, I have stopped trying to define it, at least with words. It seems that the more I try to find words to suit it, the more I am fooling myself. All I know is that the answer is within, somewhere, somehow. I don't know but it feels that even though I don't know (intellectually) I still know on some deeper level somehow. It is not even a feeling/emotion but something beyond even that, something much more certain. I guess I could call it a deep intuition, all thinking and feeling just seems to cloud that. I know that it's some sort of a connection I am trying to establish/find to something deeper within, to something that leaves un-needing of anything else. Any thoughts?

The need to find the answer within is the first great intuitional revelation. The need to define the self may be the second.

❧

I've often wondered what the connection was between body and mind...

My feeling is that the body tumbles out of the mind (part of the mind's projection of the world of things) and that it's sort of a two-way pulsation, with percepts hitting the mind from the world of things. The mind is like a two-headed Janus, with inputs coming both from the world of things it projects and also from its source. I'd say that its primary attention is directed only in one direction at a time—either "outward" to the inputs coming from the world of things, which includes body stuff, or "inward" toward its source. Inward-focused attention provides data that conflicts with the self-beliefs that accumulate. At some point the two result in prolonged conscious conflict.

❧

I resist the urge to write you most days. I frequently open your book and find the answer to my question(s) and know that my questions are probably not very relevant to what I need to be doing.... which is surrendering and letting go... both of which seem to be really difficult for me.

The weekend of 7/13, I went to an Adyashanti retreat outside Philly and last weekend, I went to an Anam Thubten retreat in Princeton. Both were very profound, but what I find is that my clarity seems more clear and my confusion seems more opaque and the cycle time is rapid and violent... in other words, I am not abiding in awareness or anything else other than my own BS....

I am feeling frustrated and annoyed. Any advice?

PS: I also meant to mention that last night I watched a beautiful Spanish film called "The Sea Inside" about a quadriplegic man who wanted to end his life and was ultimately successful. What seems to be true is that I am more attracted to death than waking up. There was a man who was killed when a tree fell on his car near here a week ago and I was envious. I don't really feel suicidal but I do feel hopeless and I want out. When I try to find a reason to go on, I feel more disabled than a quadriplegic.

If we watch the way a child surrenders or lets go of a toy and then bring it to an adult level... more complicated reactions, perhaps, but it seems to me the same motivations are at play: tired of the toy, falling asleep, having it yanked out of his grip, getting attracted to something more appealing, etc.

I think we're incapable of surrendering but capable of being overwhelmed. Surrendering to the truth is being overwhelmed by the truth.

Doubt is our ally in the duel with faulty beliefs. As is faith. Doubt and faith are not opposed; they operate on different levels.

Eventually we get to the point where mind activity either subsides or otherwise stops interfering with observation.

Then, if we're still actively listening/looking/feeling for the truth of self, we may find it.

In the meantime, our intuition will tell us the next step or give us a feel for what's needed.

What level of mind subsidence did you witness during the Adyashanti and Anam retreats? What does "clarity more clear" mean to you? Does your mind get to a point of focusing on your main inquiry?

My advice is still basically the same... follow your intuition, for which we have to get quiet enough to hear. It's Blatvatsky's "voice of silence," Bob Fergeson's "listening attention," Richard Rose's "invisible current"... the angels descending Jacob's ladder.

A reason to go on? Well, since life isn't rational, you're asking for a lot. :-) Look to feeling... What's your deepest desire?

If it's: "More of the same (e.g., another life)... no, thanks," then play the odds: we honestly don't know what death will bring. Make optimum use of existence. Find the Truth/first know thyself and see if that resolves the problem.

❧

Most of the time I feel filled with pervasive fear of what's outside me and inside me, of the past, present and future. I want to be saved. I want to be saved from myself.

I know what you mean. That was my position for many years, too. I've been going through my journals, and I see that I was treated to a lot of suffering, like you. And like a large percentage of humanity, I suspect. I think, though, that I was in love with my suffering, which might be what prolonged the awakening process (and being saved from myself; there are still emotionally painful times in my life, but the pain no longer threatens annihilation). I'm reminded of a remark that Tess Hughes made to one of the guys in the Pittsburgh group: "The content of the mind isn't important." To awaken, I'm rather sure that thoughts—and by that, I mean mental movement in general, including feelings, etc.—have to not interfere with observation. That can happen if thought either stops or can be ignored. A simple meditation would be to practice ignoring thought.

※

Tell me everything you know about fear. :-) I'm inclined to dissect its feeling right now.

The short form: Fear has practical purposes. The trick may be learning to distinguish practical fear from fear that interferes with what we want to accomplish.

Looking at the flip side of the coin, i.e., desire, suppose for example that I want to live with somebody I love who loves me but doesn't want to live with me. What is "right action" for me? If I step back and look at the desirability of the possible outcomes, I may see that:

- Based on the criterion of my personal happiness, "live with" may be better.

- Based on the criterion of my effectiveness in helping others, "don't live with" may be better.

- Based on the criterion of the other person's unfolding, "don't live with" may be better.

My discriminating faculty may jump to a set of actions that supports one side or the other, or it may tell me to watch and wait for a sign of right action.

We may be able to flip the coin over and get a reading on fear by stepping back and looking at the desirability of possible outcomes based on how we react to the fear.

✄

My current state of mind regarding the path [is] that I feel utterly lost, uncertain and stuck on and about it and existence in general.

Everyone is lost until they're "found" — i.e., awaken. The ones who admit it to themselves, rather than running around in circles or self-medicating, etc., are fortunate. They may panic initially, then sink into a period of despair. But despair may eventually lead to clearer thinking about action to maximize the possibility of being rescued or finding their own way home.

Think about your son, for example, getting lost on a wilderness hike when he's older. What are the productive actions he could take? He could set a course by the sun, follow a stream, call out at regular intervals, build signal fires at night, remind himself that although there's no guarantee of success he won't regret putting his attention on his objective, and so on. Could you construct a similar action plan for becoming unlost?

Each wilderness-survival action might have a parallel action for finding the Peace that outwits mortality.

✄

How can I let go of control? The I is struggling with the thought that if it lets go—all manner of hell will break loose—like someone will die, etc. Now, intellectually, I know that what is going to happen is going to happen no matter what. The struggle is being watched and I'm praying to surrender. Got any good pointers?

Thanks by the way for helping me out—I'm pretty over the moon about it.

That's a conviction shared by, I would guess, about 99% of humanity. And we can see it's useful for survival purposes; otherwise, we'd all be walking in front of trucks and taxicabs.

The idea of letting go of control is probably a reaction to a feeling that it would be the solution to ending stress. The mind works in terms of opposites, which is a practical way to counteract symptoms but doesn't always get at underlying problems.

How do you know that whatever is going to happen is going to happen? A fatalistic belief doesn't prove fatalism. Just as the mind justifies worrying by "logic" that says: "I worried about the sky falling yesterday, and it didn't fall; ergo, worrying worked," a feeling when looking back that "nothing could have been different" doesn't say anything about whether the future has been woven yet. We don't know, so an agnostic position with regards to fatalism is most honest. (These are just my opinions, of course. :-) The serenity prayer may be a more objective prayer—a little computer asking the Big Computer for guidance.

A practical, as opposed to neurotic, type of worrying may take the form of: "What reasonable things should I do to prepare for a possible power outage?" It starts by doing a triage to determine: "Where can I invest my limited energy or effort most wisely?"

Don't panic—work. Work productively. Find ways to let the body relax and reduce stress, sure. Allow the mind to find some quiet respites, sure. But to get at the underlying problem of stress, we have to find the answer to: "Who's got the stress?" Stress is the symptom; the underlying problem is not knowing what we truly are.

Until then we're lost in the wilderness. Admitting that to ourselves is the starting point for productive work. Initially we may panic, and then we may sink into hopelessness. But hopelessness may eventually lead to clearer thinking, and then to action. We can set a path by orienting with the sun. We can follow a stream. We can call out at regular intervals. We can build signal fires at night. We don't know if our actions will be effective, but we won't have any regret knowing that we put our attention on our objective and worked toward it.

Sacred Ivy—by Corina Baldasuc
Used for the cover of the *Meetings with Remarkable Women DVD*
produced by *PoetryInMotionFilms.com.*

Of Goats & Gates

irst, I'd like to try to convey a general perspective:

- You're here, conscious of individual existence, for a purpose, and that purpose is to know yourself.

- You are not [your name goes here]. You are what you always have been and always will be. You are that which was never born, never dies.

- You couldn't accomplish your purpose if the happy button were stuck in the "on" position. Your unhappiness, suffering, and misery are great gifts that can lead to Full Satisfaction.

- Desiring an end to suffering now, desiring instant satisfaction, is good. Knowing yourself is instantaneous, beyond time.

- Pursuing self-knowing—your job, your real purpose—as a conscious goal and as your life-priority is surrendering to the Self. (Thy will, not mine, be done.) Your self-consciousness, your I-amness, is the clue that can be followed back to the Source.

- [Your name goes here] will surrender in the final analysis. It can be done the hard way or the easy way, but in the end, every individual is going to lose the battle. Thankfully.

Now, to get a little more specific, I'll tell you about my experience while living on a farm many years ago. There was a herd of goats there, whose job (although they didn't know it) was to keep the multiflora rose bushes and other brush from taking over. In the summer they roamed freely, although we had the farm fenced in sections to keep them in and to keep the wild dogs out. In the winter, they would go out foraging in the day, but then we kept them in a barn at night and fed them. Getting them back to the barn might mean having to get them through a fence gate, depending on where they were.

Trying to herd them through the gate from behind was an exercise in futility. They'd pretend they didn't see the gate and would run one way or the other along the fence line rather than go through. The only way I found to get them through before they were ready (if they ever were) was to be on the other side of the gate with some corn—like candy to them—in a can and to rattle it around to get their attention. Then they'd rush through the gate, stampeding to see who could get through first, entirely willing to trample me down to get at the corn.

The moral of the story: The teacher can't push us through the gate. The Self entices us through when we realize it's The Way to satisfy our greatest desire.

What Banged?

If the cosmos began with a big bang, what banged? What was already "here" to bang? If particles (pieces of something, matter, physical substance), where did the *first* particle come from? If potential, it was a latent quality or capability of what? Energy is defined as the capacity of a physical system to perform work (i.e., movement of other physical systems). Potential energy is defined as the energy of a body or system due to its position relative to others, stresses within itself, electric charge, etc. Energy depends on things moving.

"As scientists know now, the universe is constantly expanding. As you move backward in time, then, the universe contracts. Rewind far enough (about 13.8 billion years), and the entire universe shrinks to the size of a single atom, Hawking said."

Back to the problem: where did that single atom come from?

Manna V

You'll know when you've reached a new form of knowing, self-knowing. It is different from any kind of knowing you've experienced.

And with that new knowing, you'll unknow any other certainty.

You'll become your own authority on knowing and unknowing.

You'll know when you've reached a new state of being, absolute being. Self-knowing is absolute being.

❧

There's no such thing as a true self-belief. On the surface, you might expect that the belief "I'm something beyond consciousness, something that exists when the body is in dreamless sleep, etc." may be a true belief. But it's like a belief in nonduality: The belief and the believer of the belief are contradictory.

❧

Defining the self means answering the one ultimately important question of life and death: "Who or what am I?"

❧

All you need to do is find the real self among all the pretenders. Nothing complex.

❧

Loving (people, animals, god) is one side of the equation. In a way it's the easier side, as I'm sure is either wrong or you already know. :-) Receiving love from people and feeling god's love is often harder. We react with fear of losing ourselves, fear of being overwhelmed, obligations, and so on. Both sides of the equation contain the belief in self and other. And then there's *being* love… our origin and destination.

❧

Regarding ego death: self-knowing doesn't dissolve the ego, defining ego as the sense of I-amness. More accurately, "ego death" is a term describing the death of the conviction of *individual* selfhood, the belief that "I am something."

❧

The mind isn't constructed to conceive of the ALL, which would have to be both all good and all evil, and neither. The true self is the ALL.

Of course that's just my testimony, and hearsay isn't admissible evidence in the court of self-inquiry. The court of self-inquiry backs into the truth of self by seeing through mistaken identity. The self-inquiring mind has to see (intuitively) the truth of what we're not and accept (intuitively) the implications, which break the tie with faulty identity.

❧

If the feeler rejects all thought as relevant, he's a feeling fool. Similarly, if the thinker rejects all feeling as irrelevant, he's a thinking fool.

❧

Regardless of how philosophically sophisticated we become, we can't outwit our painful sense of separation in/with the mind. But then I have to contradict myself. :-) Somehow the mind can consciously come into contact with its source. The mind is projected from its source, and the mind picks up that connection in nostalgia or longing, but becoming conscious of its source is a major discontinuity. The Self knows the mind, and when the conscious connection opens, the mind bows to Lord Self.

❧

The mental computer works to solve the biggest problem currently on its plate. And the biggest of all, always in the background even if not in the foreground, is SURVIVAL. And of course the biggest antagonist is DEATH.

All experience becomes grist for the survival mill. And the computer will calculate probabilities of whether the different experiences are useful for its survival.

The determination always comes down to what horse(s) to place our money on. The race we're talking about is the race with death… and the time frame is ambiguous. Even people with diagnoses of stage 4 cancers seem to be unable to escape procrastination and distraction.

"I'll get to it later" may not turn out to have been a good strategy.

❧

Reviewing my 26 years of journals reminded me that my meditation practice was full of ups and downs (mainly the latter), offs and ons, and I never felt that it got me anywhere. And yet I suspect that it developed a sort of muscle so that when I witnessed the final opposition—consciousness of awareness—I continued staring at it for a sufficient period. One thing for sure: the only thing we can truly know for sure is what we truly are. Anything else falls squarely into the realm of speculation.

❧

The mind is a problem-solving machine, and it will follow its nose.

❧

Impractical? Awakening is facing the ultimate practical reality.

❧

What clouds the view all the way up to the final breakthrough are the faulty beliefs we have about what we are. Somehow these beliefs have to come into view and then be contrasted to other views that appeal to us as possibly true. That shedding of the delusion of knowing occurs naturally in life, but the job of the conscious seeker is to look for ways of accelerating the process.

- Corral a self-belief.
- Look for evidence that contradicts that belief.

Ambrosia V

The idea of watching the mind to gain detachment from its competing claims and locus of identification seems to focus on what is consciously available. What about the unconscious forces in ourselves which are holding us prisoner? Is there any way to bring these into view besides dreams?

I'm not sure what you mean by unconscious forces in ourselves that are holding us prisoner. We can become conscious of every percept hitting the mind, whether it's coming in from what might be reactions to projections of the mind (i.e., sensory input) or coming in from another channel, which is probably what people refer to as our 6th sense. We know nothing for sure about the source of any of those percepts We can speculate that they're from other life forms like cats and trees and people, or from invisible life forms like angels, devils, and other entities, or directly from the Big Computer, and it may be helpful to discern the possible source, but we're still dealing in the realm of probability. We can also become conscious of all the mind's operations although I don't believe either is necessary. What keep us "prisoners in the mind" are the beliefs in our limitations, and we'll hold onto them until we see contrary evidence that convinces the jury otherwise... and then the mind-fist will open to the Absolute.

Investigate what you believe yourself to be... not some grandiose definition but the "little" convictions. We have to get behind or "see through" our identification with personhood and then come up against our belief in individuality.

Do you know of any tips or practices that may help me trust others more?

Trust and love may be very closely related in terms of how they function. We open the heart, letting down our defenses. It's a vulnerable position, risky. We choose something other than fear, relaxing our assertion of control, maybe overriding our will to power.

Feelings are the problem? Does that give you any clues to your current self-definition?

Well, the feelings are not the problem themselves, I think happiness/contentment exists with whatever is going on. That I am the feeler? I do believe in this, that I am somehow responsible for feeling the way I do, that somehow I should be able to change it if I could, the emotion I mean.

I never got the meaning of these questions, mostly it just ends up in intellectual ponderings and more thought about thought. These "I" questions annoy me a bit because I don't seem to be getting the point of them. Could you expand on this a little, Art?

Unless we're at the point where we can reverse the direction of the inquiry vector to aim directly at Truth, or it reverses for us, we back away from untruth. Since the quest of self-inquiry is a search for self, backing away from untruth involves questioning what we currently feel/believe ourselves to be. We look for something specific to question, and then we look for evidence that may undermine the belief. What do you currently believe yourself to be? Or, where is the current dividing line between self and not self? Is it true? We need to look until the evidence shifts the dividing line.

✲

The insights that came up during the healing retreat feel true to me, but I recognize that they are perceptual filters (new beliefs). I wonder how this might fit into the path to enlightenment. This question has been on my mind a lot but so far, I haven't found an answer. I had a strong intuition to go there, and feel that healing of some problems really did happen. But I also feel a bit confused because I resonated so strongly with healing (I actually cried from gratitude while giving healings). I could take it as a sign that healing is something to explore more, but I'm very hesitant as I don't want to waste time deviating from the path to enlightenment. What do you say about this?

It may help to step back and look at the criteria we're using to judge the desired outcomes of our actions. For example, suppose I felt a desire to become a healer. On the basis of feeling gratitude, putting resources into the endeavor might be "good." On the basis of helping others, it's "risky" predicting what is best for another person. On the basis of what's best for me, how would I know that until I know the knower? So I'd have to try to gauge it in terms of whether it appeals to me as the most realistic path to self-knowing.

Warren Buffett, one of the most successful investors to date, has a philosophy of waiting for fat pitches, a baseball term, implying that he doesn't act often. He watches and waits for opportunities that ring his bell. He makes big commitments and sticks with them. If we're going to follow any path, we have to be committed to stick on it long enough to see where it will take us. There are a minimum number of paths we can go down among the multitude to choose from.

We need to discern carefully and commit fully to any path that we feel may take us where we want to go.

※

A little background. Douglas Harding's readings and experiments didn't work for me, frustration. Am just finishing Bob Fergeson's book.

So I came from nothing, I'm going to nothing when body dies, I am nothing behind all these illusions.

So is the point to remember this and that is it?

How do you go on with this life experience knowing it is for not? (Not suicidal, just disillusioned.)

Harding's experiments are trying to show a new way of looking at things. So we have to suspend our disbelief in seeing in a new way. For example, we've all been conditioned to believe that our feet are "down" when we're standing or sitting. That's due to assuming there's a horizontal line extending out from our eyes ("the horizon"), and anything below that line is "down" while anything above it is "up." This conditioned interpretation is what Harding refers to as a 3rd person, or learned, view.

But we, the viewer, can see nothing behind us in the view. From that standpoint, there's nothing "behinder" or "belower" or "downer" than us. Anything in our view is "up" from where we, the viewer, are. The torso that's in the view is "up" regardless of the position the body is in. Same for the arms, hands, legs, feet, etc. It's a different paradigm, based on different assumptions. Neither paradigm may be ultimately true, but both may be equally valid ways of interpreting what we see.

I don't think you know what you are, or where you came from before birth, or where you'll go or what you'll become after you die, do you? It's not something we can get any mileage out of by taking someone else's word for. We have to find out for ourselves in order to settle the mind. If somebody says you're "nothing," why would you believe that? If somebody says you're "an eternal soul," why would you believe that? Alfred Pulyan, a Zen master, told Richard Rose: "Nothing of you will remain" after death. Notice carefully: he didn't say nothing would remain. He said "nothing of you" would remain. I can tell you that he meant "nothing of what you currently believe yourself to be" will remain, but again just believing what somebody says doesn't do the trick.

The point is to find out for yourself. "Look for yourself" as Harding said. "Observe the observer" in Rose's terms.

How do you know that life has no purpose? Rose used to say that the human population could be divided into two groups, those who believed that life is a bordello and those who believed it's a schoolhouse. I like the former interpretation but believe the latter. :-)

The purpose of life, in my view, could be called love. If it's a schoolhouse, I don't think the purpose is to learn how to perfect ourselves, how to outdo the neighbors, etc. In my view, the whole story is Love becoming love becoming Love. Love—or the All (our true identity)—projects individuality. The individual loves herself or himself first. If we're lucky, we fall in love with another person (often with our children), and the distinction between self and other vanishes for a moment or two. This is an occurrence of the mind (or heart-mind) opening. When that occurs, the fears and desires start yammering, and the heart-mind eventually closes to some degree. The culmination of this process, which may occur before or during death, is that the heart-mind opens fully and our identification transcends self-other. We consciously become "the All," the Unconditional, the Eternal Love that we've always been looking for.

PS: I go through emotional ups and downs like everybody. The difference being that, once we know what we truly are, life's slings and arrows no longer threaten us at the core of our conscious being. I remember one time when I called Richard Rose, I asked him how he was. There was silence on the other end of the line, then he replied: "You stopped my head." It's a funny (funny-strange and funny-ha ha), paradoxical situation when we know what we are.

This brain accepts the point of Harding's games, that he wants you to question learned concepts. This brain has been undergoing paradigm shifts for years now. I'm getting a little hung up on the observe the observer. So get behind C. and observe her or C. observe the things that happen out of nowhere?

My nothing descriptions from my original email are what is experienced when this body quiets. And you are right, it is more I don't know than nothing about the pre-birth and death experience.

I do feel my life has been more a schoolhouse and I'm with you that love is the all. So just live IT? Practice IT? Or am I still to quest for IT between the breaths?

The spiritual search ultimately goes to the root of our existence. There have been various terms used over the centuries to try to point toward the goal or end of the search such as nirvana, liberation, awakening, and self-realization. They all relate to one or the other side of the finding-losing coin: losing our illusory beliefs about what we really are or finding what we truly are.

Questions that try to get at the end goal of the search include: Who or what am I? What was I or where did I come from before birth? What will I become or where will I go after death? What is the source of my consciousness or awareness?

Rose was a unique teacher or helper, in my view, based on his broad prescription of how to get to the end of the search.

He described *mind* as the entire dimension of existence and pointed out its schizoid or dualistic nature. In this dimension there is no absolute point of reference. We can only know something in terms of its opposite. And yet we're all looking, consciously or unconsciously, for absolute X, which our different mentalities may think of as Wholeness, Completion, Reality, Never-ending Satisfaction, Unconditional Love, Truth, Eternal Security, and so on.

How do we use our dualistic tools—thought and feeling, let's call them—to transcend dualism? How do we get beyond the limitations of the dualistic mind to find what we're looking for? We don't know how to find X, our true nature or Self. But what we can do is back away from our illusory beliefs of what we are. To do that, we need to work with some arbitrary distinction between self and not-self. For example, knower vs. known, view vs. viewer, or observer vs. observed: the self that we're looking for is the *knower*, and anything that we know is not-self; the unknown self is the *viewer*, and anything in the view is not-self; or what we are is the *observer*, and anything observed is not-self. We can then consider the end of the search as knowing the knower, viewing the viewer, or observing the observer—ending the split or limitation of dualism and finding the absolute condition that we're looking for, if that's possible.

In order to work at the process of self-inquiry leading to self-realization, Rose suggested using the paradigm of inside vs. outside to distinguish between where we currently believe ourselves to be and where we truly are. In other words, the unknown knower (viewer, observer, self) is *inside*, and anything in the view (seen, known, etc.) is *outside*. Outside, or not self, includes trees, people, our viewed or felt body, our thoughts, our feelings, and our mental processes such as decision-making. We cannot *look* or feel inside to find the self, since anything that's in the view (seen or felt with our six senses) is outside the self. We look or feel to distinguish what is not self, and that leads to our "going within" to find or become the absolute self-truth-love.

As far as living it, practicing it, questing for it between the breaths: yes. The closest thing that comes to mind is a blank-verse poem I used as an epilogue in *Solid Ground of Being* titled "Don't Be Afraid":

Don't be afraid to love.
Yes, it will open you to disappointments and rejections,
But it will free you from the lockdown of solitary confinement.
Behind it is the desire to become one with,
And behind that is the vague memory of where we come from
And how we got here.
We came out of Perfection, of Perfect Love,
Through the doorway of mental love,
Of being one with our mother's mind.
Then, if we were fortunate, through the transition
Of parental affection as we matured
Into the realization of physical separation.
We long to return to The Perfection,
But we're seemingly imprisoned in individuality,
In separation.
The return journey may take us back through physical love,
The unity of touch; through mental love, the unity of rapport;
Through cosmic love, unity with all things.
In the end, our journey from Love to Love
Will take us back to the realization of oneness with
What we always have been and ever will be.

❧

I had an attack of chronic boredom. It's happened before but I usually have some sort of reason for it (like PMS or something) but today I had none of that and it had me by the throat. I had the whole day to myself so I was planning to just relax and read and do the things I looked forward to, but for some reason again this familiar sucky feeling came over me, it's hard to describe, a feeling of "not wanting." It's not depression, that feels different. This feeling was more like an irritation, like a restlessness that would not go away and it just confounded me because it came with a strong conviction that there is NOTHING to be done about it... not one book, or walk or internet browsing or anything. I guess it's chronic boredom; ok when I am describing it now it almost does sound like depression. Hmmm. So anyway, I was caught in a bind because I had a strong feeling or boredom (which by nature requires you to extinguish it with an interest or something, because it's so uncomfortable and negative) and then I had a strong conviction that I had no desire to do anything, and nothing could be done about the boredom. So I wrestled with that for a few hours at home, kind of agonizing. Saw clearly the process of the mind deciding between which activities would be more entertaining and rejecting one by one, and then struggling to come up with more options, just to shut them down.

"I had a strong conviction that I had no desire to do anything, and nothing could be done about the boredom. So I wrestled with that for a few hours at home...." —and that's what you *did* (i.e., the internal agonizing).

When the nothing-to-be-done conviction returns in the future, you can either let a similar response play out, or you can determine *now* that you'd like a different response to occur—for example, to pursue something creative (like drawing, painting, doodling, whatever) even though you won't feel like it, just to let things take a different path. It might be instructive to notice your reaction to that suggestion. It gets down to the conflict between a desire to reshape things and "freedom" to react in the old patterns, doesn't it?

So then I was like "Hmm, it must be a mood thing, that's why I don't want to do anything, so in order to change my desires I have to change my mood." So I drank a beer, which luckily my boyfriend keeps our fridge stocked with. :-) That did nothing, except make me dizzy for a while, but no respite from the irritating "not wanting" and not knowing what to do next. So you could say well what's so wrong with this not wanting, sounds good to me. Yes, it sounds like it would be, but the problem was that it was an irritating "not wanting," as if it was pushing me to do something, anything, and i just didn't know what. So I was at a loss for direction, because my desires give me direction for my next movement, and I had none. So I was stuck.

"My desires give me direction for my next movement...." —in other words, you're enslaved to whatever desire presents itself at the moment. Is that the way you want to live and die? Can you discern some desires that are more important to you than others and learn to let them take precedence in shaping your action?

🌿

I had a couple questions about this week's comment you sent to me [Have you tried Rose's suggestion of launching a message to the inner self when you begin a meditation session: "I'd prefer to think of nothing rather than tolerate rambling thoughts"?] *I really like the idea of preferring to think of nothing rather than tolerating rambling thoughts. So after this command is given and I begin my meditation should i stick to focusing on my breath and looking away from thoughts or should I just try and turn my internal head away from the thought and think of nothing? Would a place to put my attention be useful or would that be "thinking of something." Should I consciously attempt to think of nothing? How should i proceed with the actual meditation?*

We don't control thinking directly, Mike. By consciously watching whatever's going on, we can learn to control the mind indirectly, by "turning the inner head" away from mind activity that's not relevant to what we're trying to focus on. That's the trick to studying or writing an essay, for example, when we're being bombarded by other desires. It's a very casual thing... not fighting or suppressing the contrary urges but acknowledging and procrastinating them. That's the entire procedure for bringing the mind under control to the extent it may be possible.

The directive or reminder or "order to the computer" that we'd prefer to think of nothing rather than tolerate rambling thoughts (including thoughts and feelings that aren't relevant to the objective we're trying to focus on during the session) is an assertion that we'll be okay if there's no thought, if thought just stops for a while.

As a separate exercise, you could try the experiment of thinking about nothing... and note what occurs. But that's definitely not what Rose is getting at by his description. If thought stops, either while meditating or at another time, you won't do anything other than what you've always done and only do, which is to observe.

You are *never* that which you observe or experience... not the body moving, not the thought that directs muscle movement, not the decision-making that precedes action, not the emotions you experience. You don't take credit for the doing of the autonomic nervous system. Similarly, you're not doing the rest of the neural system's processing. All thought is reaction.

If thought stops, proceed with meditation the same way all meditation occurs... by consciously watching. Meditation is watching until the observer is observed. That cannot occur within the limitations of the mind dimension. You will then know the truth about your essential nature or being and will have an entirely new and radical perspective on life, love, and death.

🌿

Lately I have been feeling so frustrated, so out of sorts that I don't want to write, to read, to meditate, anything.

This morning I was looking through my notebook I keep in my truck to record thoughts while driving, and it seems that ever since I hit on the thought that "I am not the awareness that I think I am"... I have been lost and feeling more lost each day. I venture to say that I am feeling somewhat depressed as well. Today is a struggle to go to work. Ego is struggling to be heard, silence has taken a back seat. My gut says to allow this to take its course. Just looking for your thoughts...

It's both simple and complex, Mike. Simple when we know what we are but complex before the mind opens to the Truth.

From the mind's perspective, we're the aware subject that we can't see. That's the frustration, that we can't see ourselves. All certainty depends on seeing/knowing what we are. Uncertainty = frustration. It's a seemingly impossible situation... and yet it's somehow possible to see/know what we are.

Getting to the point where we admit to ourselves that we've tried everything we can think of and it hasn't worked is the fun-effort part. Then we keep working despite the seeming hopelessness of if... and something happens, if it's in the cards. If we assume it's in the cards, we're kidding ourselves. If we assume it's not in the cards, we're kidding ourselves.

🌿

The previous email led me to a thorough reading of the Benoit recap
page on your site.[21] I really like his compensation framing of the
games we play, but I have a hard time accepting that acceptance
through humility is the way out. :-)

Benoit was savvy enough to state that humility is *the* way
but not *a* way. It's what occurs, but it's not something we
do. It occurs from 1) seeing something about self/other that's
relatively truer than what we previously believed, and 2)
accepting the truth rather than not facing it. Those insights
or disillusionments are always going to be deflating, which
is why they're humbling.

There's a passage in the Gospel of John that describes
this diminishment in a poetic way: "The bride belongs to
the bridegroom. The friend who attends the bridegroom
waits and listens for him, and is full of joy when he hears
the bridegroom's voice.... He must become greater; I must
become less."[22]

A son of man becomes less when he loves another and
when he sees himself becoming his father.

❧

You always say you like hearing my glimpses or insights. So this
hit me I think yesterday, and I just wrote this for AR[23]:

I feel like it has finally sunk in what is in the way. The core
fear is exactly the same as the desired end result. I am afraid
of realizing what I really am, of a final unity or oneness (all-
oneness, or aloneness) of whatever happens to the sense of Judy.

---

21   www.selfdiscoveryportal.com/BenoitZen.htm
22   John 3:29-30
23   An email accountability/confrontation group monitored by Anima
     Pundeer.

I'm afraid that I really am God, or afraid of what that would feel like. It's as if I need faith in the idea that awakening is desirable.

I've been puzzling over your "2000 conviction state" piece ever since you sent it. I can see that it made sense in 2000. I would think most people have felt much the same for at least a portion of their lives. But in the end, I don't think I have the perspective needed to see how it fits into who you are at this point.

It's an interesting conundrum, isn't it. I came across a good wording for it in a detective novel (yep, I've recently resurrected an entertainment form from decades past): "Are you afraid of becoming nothing or are you afraid of being nothing?"

The organism of experience—the body-mind that we're identified with before we find what we really are—is graced with fears and desires to keep it functioning. The intuition program of that organism tells it that looking back through the projector, looking into its source, threatens its existence. That's the fear side of the message. The desire side of intuition's message is that looking back into its source will yield ultimate fulfillment. That's the generic form of the final opposition or set of opposites to be transcended.

If the experience-organism continues to function after self-recognition, it will still operate based on habitual reaction patterns, fears and desires, intuition, changing moods, and conviction state(s). The only difference for the organism is that the bedrock conviction of what's experiencing will have changed. The organism now knows that it's not what experiences—a vast, paradoxical contradiction. Another way to express it is that we then know that we're not affected by experience.

You probably recall hearing or reading Richard Rose's reference to the old Zen saying that before enlightenment, mountains are mountains… and after enlightenment, mountains are once again mountains.[24] Before I knew what I am, I loved sweets. After knowing what I am, Art still loves sweets.

๛

In what way do you see the value in investigating "I Am-ness"? I understand that it serves to cut off the multiple identities we assume ourselves to be. But I've heard it said so often, there is no "I" to begin with. So is this just an intermediate exercise until the impersonal witness takes center stage, preparing the way for the final Reality to be recognized?

The impersonal witness is already center stage and has been since time began. The mind's reaction to the impersonal witness, to consciousness, is I-amness. The mind can't help it; it's how the mind is structured. "No fault" as the *I Ching* spreads copiously throughout its commentary if I remember right. All there is, is I. (Not I-amness, which is only a seeming… but is the doorway.)

๛

I do have a depth of sincerity for mental freedom, yet I still feel closed off… I want to participate sometimes, yet my default reaction is to not… not participate, not volunteer, not initiate… sometimes this fear is gone and not an issue. I see fear when the closed-off reaction is there… not pride. I can't tackle this problem in the normal way

---

24   "Before I sought enlightenment, the mountains were mountains and the rivers were rivers. While I sought enlightenment, the mountains were not mountains and the rivers were not rivers. After I attained enlightenment, the mountains were mountains and the rivers were rivers." Author unknown.

yet because it is too close for me to see it clearly. How can I get a step away from this problem or be free of it?

The watching (of defensive reaction) can occur both while it's happening and in later review. If the mind computes that the reaction isn't to its advantage in certain situations, it can react with determination to react differently in those situations in the future. If it does react differently, then there will be more data collected from the experiment. If not, if the defensive reactions continue in situations where you'd like to see them change, then the mind may react with renewed determination to see them change.

If a meditation practice, for example, or any repetitive experience leaves a peaceful feeling, then it may be valuable as a means of relaxation. Some of that is obviously needed by everyone... hence the value of play or even work that leaves us tired but relaxed. But to stir the mind to inquire, to doubt, irritation is necessary. Discomfort. The mind is constantly computing the pros and cons of any reaction, and over time, various fears and desires get different weightings in the decision-making. Fear says move away, desire says move closer.

❧

If it is true that we had no beginning, why is it that we have no inkling or postmonition(?) of some awareness before birth?

Speak for yourself. :-) The types of knowing you're familiar with (perception and conception) occur in various states of consciousness, which are operating through a projected organism. There's a third form of knowing, which occurs beyond time, and which consciousness can participate in.

When that happens, we know what we are before birth, during life, and after death.

❦

In response to the question: "What do you need to be ready for death?" a friend replied:

> If it isn't the attainment of seeing the Light, then at least I want to have made peace with my life and self. With the waste of regrets, guilt, and other debris cleared away as much as possible. I want to have some kind of certainty that my creator understands I only wanted to know him intimately, and am sincerely sorry for whatever I did or didn't do which prevented this. That I did my best to learn from mistakes and make amends for them however possible.

You and your creator have never been not-one. You-and-your-creator is what experiences knowing and not knowing. When are you going to drop the charade of being separate from yourself? When are you going to look away from personal drama long enough to recognize yourself? Intuition processes feeling but is not affected by it. Thoughts and feelings tell you otherwise, but intuition knows that "attainment of seeing the Light" is nothing other than being what you've always been.

❦

I penned the following thoughts about how retreat participants had responded to a five-minute writing exercise based on the theme: "I am....", with protests from one of the participants interspersed in italics:

Do you head yourself off from the corral of looking with an "I don't know" reaction? Of course you don't know;

otherwise, there would be no need for investigation. But if that's a stopping point for you,

Stopping point... perhaps. But perhaps not.

you've followed a path of the tired, the hopeless, the paranoid, or some other sense that the threat of looking would overwhelm you.

Suggestions of the above perhaps... but again perhaps not.

But how could that be the case? What were you afraid you might see, and why would that threat shut down your investigation?

Could it be "I don't know" actually means "I don't know?" Could it be that whatever the mind comes up with for an answer of "self," "me," or "I" doesn't pass the test. What test? If it is in the view, it isn't me. I then becomes what sees... so what sees that? The echo of the self, the sense of I am-ness is also in the view... and not the viewer.

Right... that's where logic goes into spin cycle. Logic is only as good as the starting assumptions. It's those feeling-beliefs of what we are that have to come into consciousness.

As Richard Rose pointed out—and his bias may be different from Ramana's or Nisargadatta's, definitely different from Harding's—you can't get there directly until preliminaries occur. The homework involves backing away from untruth. The probably-obscure convictions we have about what we are must come into conflict with more likely convictions, and we "trade up" to improve our collection or team. Eventually we get to a "most valuable player"... and then that MVP has to come into doubt. That was my path, and therefore the one I'm in the best position to comment on.

Instead of following the apparent default programming of looking for evidence to support our beliefs, as seekers we need to look for evidence that brings them into doubt.

Mired in Experience

Take a step back.
You are that which experiences, not that which you experience.

You are not sometimes hot, sometimes cold; sometimes happy, sometimes unhappy; sometimes hungry, sometimes full.

Step back into silence—into the silence from which you witness life, and from which you will witness death.
You are not that which was born and will die.

When you witness what you are, you will know your relationship to life and death.

"I'd Pray for You"

I'd pray for you,
But praying would confuse my mind
Past repair, past despair…
Maybe causing a tsunami
That would wash out the universal shore.
And then where would you be,
With no land to crawl out of the ocean onto....

Atlantic shore, USA. Thanks to www.edupic.net.

Final Scattering

How do we locate a self-belief? Look for irritations. The self-beliefs that need to come into the light of consciousness are feeling-beliefs, not intellectual beliefs or conclusions, which are more superficial. A *credo* (I believe) writing exercise of "I feel superior because...." followed by "I feel inferior when...." may turn up some new insights. Approach these self-selected experiments with light-hearted curiosity.

❧

I've seen a TV show a couple of times about people who've made a lot of money deciding to give some away. They interview various prospective people or organizations, volunteer to do some work with them, then surprise them with $ gifts. There's value in accomplishment, but they find that the real joy in life is when we do something for others. It moves us in a way that accomplishment or attainment doesn't. It brings warmth rather than anticlimax. Giving is love in action. What do we have, to give?

❧

"'Truth' is not a goal in science... The major goal of science [is] explanation." — *The Brain: Big Bangs, Behaviors and Beliefs*, by Rob DeSalle & Ian Tattersall

I think that's a good description of how the mind searches for understanding. We want to find the Truth of self but keep it at arm's length from ourselves. Becoming the truth threatens our most cherished belief.

❧

In this dimension of experience, there's a split between seer and seen, hearer and heard, etc. Our self-definition in this split dimension is always the unseen seer, the unheard hearer. The mind tries to see itself like the dog chases his tail.

❧

Seekers eventually get to the point where they intuit that they're identified with a losing proposition and would like to be free of it... but the losing proposition can't free itself of itself. Maybe that's why so many of us, even before we become conscious seekers, try to lose ourselves in booze, drugs, you-name-it.

❧

Life is Love becoming love becoming Love. Life is the teacher through love, which somehow opens the mind. Even after realization. Maybe more so.

❧

A koan for shaking something loose: "What is my problem?"

❧

Comfort: what is it, and where does it come from? The word's literal meaning tells the truth: strength (fort) through coming together... ending the illusion of self-other.

Evening Songs

W*hen I think of working from the "impersonal," I think about things like "Your Will, not mine," considering/helping others, risking rejection/disappointment, and ignoring personal drama. Are these along the lines of what you mean? As long as ego is running the show, it's problematic distinguishing or keeping separate the "personal" from the "impersonal." So is it a matter of gradually testing out and crossing over into the "impersonal" (even with the "personal" still mixed in) until ego has to give way?*

I don't know what the opposite of "working from the impersonal" would be, Paul. I don't see any evidence that ego ever runs the show. Ego is part of the show, part of the machinery observed or assumed. Investigating the impersonal is a synonym for self-inquiry: looking for the source of consciousness, the source of experiencing.

We watch our life-experience as it unfolds, including the mind's reactions, the appearance of memories, etc. Part of that life-experience is the internal dialogue where "one part of the mind-self" "talks" about or even to "another part," praising or condemning it, for example. (The ego-1, ego-2 split that Alfred Pulyan describes so well.) Ego is the I-amness or whatever the mind is identified with at the moment—typically a fear or a desire, a thought or feeling, the internal judge (ego-1), etc.

I can't see how ego isn't running the show, this dream show I live, in almost every way. It took a long time to gain the epiphany where I saw the magnitude of ego's serpentine ways behind most all my suffering, if not all of it. Now ego is no longer the problem? Or are you speaking from the perspective that the Master is using the ego as a wall we finally get tired of banging our bloody head against?

Ego is the sense of self that occurs with consciousness. If that sense of self is identified with hands, then it "does" whatever hands do; if it's identified with thinking, it does whatever thoughts do, etc. What you do, and all that you do, is observe.

I've found the sincere wish occurring more frequently that I wish my Source would call me home soon, ready or not. It brings with it a strange kind of relief. I can understand better than ever before what people mean when they are tired of living and longing for the exit.

When you observe what's observing, the "I" you currently believe yourself to be loses its existential anxiety. It may be like the unmanageable, high-strung dog or child who finally gets strong guidance and love. Until then, the weight of the world has been on him. He doesn't have to die physically for that to occur. Neither do we actually die when our Source (true self) takes us home (recognizes itself). What dies is our previous illusion of self—and it's assumed limitations.

※

I think I have spent too much time not writing. I still suffer a lot feeling disconnected from the flow of life. I continually think about what the path is to the goal of life. I guess it is following intuition, watching the ego till it is thoroughly understood, and questioning the ultimate self. I think the main thing to work on besides that, is getting a purity of intent. I keep thinking there is some "trick" though, or at least some method I'm unaware of that I should be using. Anyway, as far as purity of intent, I don't know how to relax well. I'm constantly stressed because I feel I am not progressing fast enough, and when I do focus on just progressing, it seems like I'm going in many directions without really becoming more sane. With prayer and meditation I run into problems too. With prayer it always feels like the one praying is the problem, and like I am praying to something unreal, although I do sense a higher power. With meditation, it feels very forced and like its hardening the mind. It only seems to work if I do it for a few seconds, probably because if I do it longer the mind gets too involved.

I would have liked to arrive at a coherent thought in all of that rambling, but it hasn't happened. Sorry I hadn't even asked if it was OK to write out my thoughts before doing so.

Thanks for listening.

The goal of life is death. The path to death is living. This is everyman's life experience.

The idea of enlightenment is to die while living. This is for the small percentage of people who feel they must find complete satisfaction.

What dies are the faulty beliefs about what we are.

When that death of illusion occurs, it removes the existential angst of living.

Loss of illusory beliefs = increase in sanity.

Our intuition will tell us, if we listen to it, what we need to do to take a step. For me, the awakening of intuition told me that all the answers I was looking for lay *within*. The second strong visit of intuition told me: The only chance I had for mental clarity was an extended period of sexual continence. I wanted mental clarity enough that I listened to the intuitional message and acted on it.

❧

Sooo... something happened while I was looking at my source (which is probably all that it's even sort of valid to say.) It seemed I felt the aliveness, along with a definite aloneness. I would have told you I was prepared for that, but I wasn't and withdrew.

Rearranged a bit:

> I looked at my self...
> I felt my aliveness...
> Along with a definite aloneness...
> My machinery thought it was prepared for that...
> But it wasn't...
> And I turned away from me...

All movement is evanescent. Non-movement is the background upon which movement appears. Being is movement plus non-movement.

❧

> *"You are not that sense of self;*
> *you are that which experiences it."*

I'm a little confused about identifying the real self as the experiencer. To my mind that still involves movement and some form of engagement or collusion within the sphere of change.

Regarding the real self as the experiencer: the real self witnesses. From "down here" we (the real self) witness or experience objects that change in appearance or in relation to other objects, and we sometimes witness a sense of self. Our organisms react to those changes.

I've sometimes thought the Tampa area would be a nice place to live but don't know if I could handle the humidity.

What's really important is living in a community of friends and loving relationships. Friends and relationships, like climate, will never be perfect, but the rapport of self and other is what provides satisfaction of our desire for wholeness.

🌿

Can self inquiry take place in silence and non-verbally? I sometimes think I've done enough self-observation and just want to sink into the center of my being. My longing to be free and at true peace is very strong lately.

I don't have any experience of sinking into the center of my being à la Ramana Maharshi, who I believe was referring to a practice of no-thought that triggered samadhi. Sinking into the center of my being was the result of self-inquiry once I saw what my final obstacle (faulty self-belief) was. At that point I'd say self-inquiry was pure looking.

🌿

Thanks for the intro [I'd sent Mike the introduction to *Brain Lock,* by Jeffrey M. Schwartz]. *I just finished reading it, and it was pretty interesting. Do you think these same techniques could be applied to (my) depressive/anxious thoughts? I'd say that I guess they could be categorized as obsessive, but in the intro the obsessions and compulsions that he talked about seemed to be very specific in dealing with things that these people could see were totally ridiculous, but that they just couldn't help doing. It seems like when my obsessive thoughts about not being good enough, or being anxious about performance, or feeling no good come up, its very difficult to tell myself that these things aren't rooted in some truth. My mind seems to keep presenting evidence for why they are true and it feels logical when it happens. Lately, as I try to convince myself to stick with something, be it a meditation technique or anything, it feels like I know I'll just eventually fail at it anyways. This seems to make me not want to even try and make the commitment because once i start it seems inevitable that I'll eventually fail like always. This also has the effect of reinforcing this feeling of being no good. Hope you are doing well. Thanks for the intro—any comments you have would be much appreciated.*

I do think so, Mike. The technique is based on the turning of the inner head, which is like developing a muscle through exercise reps. Paul S. said he found a newer book by the same author, Jeffrey M. Schwartz: *You Are Not Your Brain: The 4-Step Solution for Changing Bad Habits, Ending Unhealthy Thinking, and Taking Control of Your Life.*

The "trick" in getting some detachment from our reaction patterns is to step back from the specific details, which are going to vary by individual, and notice the overall form that the pattern takes. The obsessive thoughts you witness about not being good enough, for example, may be thoughts in someone else about not being sufficiently appreciated, and so on. Everyone believes their thoughts and feelings are telling them something true. And the mind seems to be designed to look for evidence that supports its beliefs and biases, doesn't it? That's part of being identified with the show that we're watching/experiencing (the life of Mike, the life of Art).

Have you considered the touchstone or point of reference your mind uses in its judgments? I often recall reading about one of Einstein's simple but brilliant thought experiments—the one where two guys in space are moving toward each other. Suppose that was Mike and Art, and suppose we wanted to determine how fast we were each moving. How would we measure your speed or my speed? We would be moving at the same speed in relation to each other, right? But if there were a third point of reference, you might be moving faster or slower relative to that than I was. What would be the truth about our individual speeds? It would be unknown and unknowable unless there were an absolute point of reference.

Do you see how vastly illogical any conclusion is unless it's understood with relation to its point of reference? Let's say that Mike is moving faster than Art with respect to a particular point of reference (which itself may be moving). And suppose Art then feels inferior to Mike, with his slowness justifying his feeling of inferiority? Is the turtle inferior to the hare? The turtle may not be in any better position to judge that question than the hare is. Somehow we'd have to have a point of reference that includes turtleness and hareness from some larger perspective. But that perspective may also be limited and biased.

We can't get perspective on the paintings hanging on the wall in an art museum if we have our nose up against them. To get perspective on what we're seeing/experiencing, we have to "step back."

I recall Richard Rose saying that the basic impediment of all strugglers is a belief in their inability to accomplish. Do you see how that generic statement may describe "the life of Mike" that you're experiencing?

✢

The other day I was, guess what, watching TV, when I suddenly became aware there was no one in the room. There were sights and sounds but no "me" watching; they were just happening. I looked to see what happened to Judy and she was just like a cardboard cutout, a figure with no inside. The phrases "no one in the house" and "no inside" came to me as if I'd never read or heard them before. I didn't see any problem with the fact that I seemed to be having these thoughts even though I was a cardboard cutout with no inside, or else not in the house. What is most remarkable about it, to me, is that I've been able to recreate this "vision" (or whatever it was) after just getting quiet, particularly the "no one is here" sense.

I also seem to have let go of that "should be doing something" feeling, finally. It seems to me that it only reinforces the ego feeling. I seem to be the observer more consistently, which feels like it has replaced the "should."

When the inside is outside,
Then all things are inside....
But where does that leave Me?

If there's no Me watching,
How do I know that sights
and sounds are happening?

No one is watching....
But Me.
Me = not one.

But Me = not many.
Not one, not many.
What does that leave Me?

Nice to get a break from that "should be doing something" urge, isn't it. The mind relaxes... lets go.

❧

What do you think of Linda Clair and her emphasis on the body? Does it really matter in what order the identification with the body and mind ceases?

I puzzled over that concerning a friend who teaches effortless meditation and again with Linda, whose zazen-type meditation seems very similar. How irrational it seems to me to conclude we're not the mind first, and then proceed to investigate our materiality. Eventually it dawned on me that by "mind," they may be talking about conceptual thought. If someone experienced a lapse of conceptual thought, I could see why they might conclude it's not essential to their I-ness.

Regardless of the path we meander or stumble along to self-definition, I think the belief in our individuality is congruent with our identification with consciousness. And I doubt that we can disentangle consciousness from possible dependence on the body—unless we've witnessed the body as separate from us in something like what's been reported in some of the clinical near-death experiences. In any case, my feeling is that the only destruction or disillusionment of our identification with consciousness is transcending consciousness while consciousness is functioning.

What was the question again? (Speaking about meandering. :-) I don't think the order of disillusionments is consequential as long as we find and maintain an ego of accomplishment that carries us to the "egoless vector" stage of self-investigation. That isn't a no-ego state. Our self-inquiry continues despite our realization that it's not going to do anything for the us we believe ourselves to be.

※

In surrendering, I seem to come across what seems like a powerful energy of resistance. A resistance to letting go of the very desire to hang on to the mentations in the mind—to stick with the story.

Have you any advice? (At the same time, I realize what the "problem" is may not seem very clear).

For the sake of argument/investigation, let's say there are two types of surrender—the type that follows a decision to surrender, and the surrender of recognition. One is a reaction of the decision-making process or program running in the mind; the other is a reaction of a possibly higher-level process we might label intuition.

The decision-making program watches the wrestling among various fears and desires and acts on the result of their contest. An example: we're going to a movie with a friend... the friend wants to see a movie we're not that interested in, but the internal contest results in going with the friend's choice. Of course there was resistance, but it got overruled in the internal wrestling match. We may or may not have been consciously watching the decision-making process as it occurred.

The intuition processes a mass of experience, including associated thoughts and feelings, and arrives at a conclusion or insight. The intuitional conclusions are factored into the decision-making process... often lost in the melee because they're rather quiet compared with fears and desires, but sometimes they override the noisy voices or somehow change the weightings of the feuding fears and desires.

You mentioned specifically: "A resistance to letting go of the very desire to hang on to the mentations in the mind—to stick with the story." I interpret this as a *desire* to let go of, or not be burdened by, the type of mental activity you described. And *resistance* indicates some fear or other set of desires and fears that oppose the desire. So I'd guess that you're watching the decision-making process, or at least seeing it's conclusion, and then recalling pieces of the process.

You also asked about advice regarding the above. I'd say: Look at the motivation for wanting to surrender. It's something you're apparently identified with... something in the view that you're hypnotically tied to. Like watching a film where somebody is getting ready to open a door, and we know there's some threat behind the door. If we feel sympathetic toward the character, we'll recoil in fear; if we dislike the character, we may smile in anticipation… in either case, the seer is identified with what is seen, what is in the view. The viewer is never the view.

In my head, there's all the mental and emotional chatter which no matter what, I can not stop—okay, but then there are the deliberate questions, prayers that one asks God also inside—that I also hear, and then the silence when you listen for an answer. I also listen for that answer when I am doing something creative or hoping to say the highest and best thing to someone in a given situation. So there is the split between the conscious question and waiting for an answer, and the awareness that you are asking the question and waiting for an answer. So what the heck is going on there?

The separation (silence) between thought streams (connected worded thoughts, feelings, pictures, sounds. etc.) varies in duration. The mind is the projection from absolute being of a dualistic cosmos. The cosmos is a mixture of ups and downs, hots and colds, particles and waves, against a background of stillness. It's composed of *things* that appear when the light of awareness picks them out. We—little Pam, little Art—see what the light of awareness illuminates… and we often become lost in what we're seeing. That's what's going on :-) What we really are at the core is nothing other than absolute being.

And what is it that we are listening to, to get the answer?

Little-Pam and little-Art are experiencing mind activity. Some of that activity is questions/prayers that appear, some is the "activity" of waiting for answers, and some is activity that we interpret as answers.

To find where all questions and answers arise from, to find *the* answer to all questions, the mind-us has to become conscious of our Source. That quest is arguably the meaning and purpose of life.

To know anything for sure, we must first know the knower.

❧

There's nothing to be done.

The path of self-inquiry gets more abstract as we go along. At some point we may see or intuit that we're not the doer — that decisions get made and action occurs as a result of mind activity, but we're not what's pulling the puppet strings. Does that mean that there's nothing to be done? It might be worthwhile looking into the beliefs behind that conclusion.

I'd say there's nothing farther from the truth than the conclusion you arrived at. Is it based on feeling that hasn't been checked out by the reasoning intellect? The refined intellect sees that the deeper it looks into something, the more it always runs into paradox.

When we see that we're not "the doer," that's true from one angle but not another. It's the antidote to the belief in being the doer, but neither is absolutely true.

So what can we "do" if we're not the doer? It would have to be an indirect doing... an indirect control of mental activity by learning to turn the inner head away from selected mental activities, thus allowing openings for other activities.

❧

Your article "I am Always Right Behind You"[25] has been very impactful and I have read it a few times. But I feel stuck at that

---

25   In *Solid Ground of Being*

spot of seeing I am "no thing" without boundaries, and eternal and unmoving, but I can't, no matter what I try, seem to see I am also "everything." In other words, I can identify with the Absolute Subject but I can't identify with the objects arising within the Absolute Subject as being "one" with that same Subject.

Seeing or intuiting a new view of what we are only occurs when we have a concept of what we are and then an opposing concept arises. The trick is that we have to become conscious of what we believe ourselves to be before that conflict can appear. Jill Bolte Taylor believed she was her body-mind until her left hemisphere became flooded with blood and she lost her ability to detect edges. With her new view, she couldn't see where she stopped and other began: she felt one with everything that came into her view. I assume that's similar to Walt Whitman's cosmic consciousness and Bernadette Roberts's unitive (earlier) experience.

There is no absolute subject to identify with. That's a trap I think many people who've been exposed to advaita concepts fall into. The spiritual path, regardless of the form it takes, is a retreat from untruth. Productive focus is on what we believe ourselves to be and then subjecting that to doubt. Life does that for us, but an intentional path tries to accelerate the process.

The value of the tests for immortality that I referred to in that write-up [referencing Douglas Harding's *Little Book of Life and Death*] is that we can use them to help ferret out our current self-belief. Richard Rose referred to the path as one of self-definition, which to me is a great term. We are trying to define ourselves. And definition (in this dimension, the mind-dimension) requires comparison. Only when we hit an ultimate comparison will its resolution propel us into self-recognition.

I am not really sure if a definitive contrast in self-definition has arisen or not (as you describe). I certainly have always thought that I was the bodymind, but after working with Harding's material for about a year I have come to seriously doubt it. I seem to be stuck at the point of not knowing which one is true (either I am the bodymind and the world is real or the world is not real and just a reflection of a self-aware no thing that has no qualities or attributes). If the truth be told I really have no idea which is the correct view and this conflict bothers me a great deal. I think about it all the time and seem to flip back and forth as the days go by but there is never any definitive evidence to convince me one way or another.

When you said "there is no absolute subject" that really stopped me in my tracks. I have been exposed to a great deal of Advaita teachings but never had what I would call a definite glimpse of non-duality. William Samuel has had a big influence on me but again what he is saying is not something I know experientially but just can appreciate intellectually. Another conflict in the mind. Although a part of me "wants" to believe him and Harding. But I guess wanting to believe it is far from knowing it.

The seeking has been really, really intense the past three years. The mind relentlessly strategizes about the way to "get there" (e.g. satori or self-recognition) but no matter what I try it fails. I fail again and again. And this has left me feeling incredibly depressed at times (in fact most days). I really wish I could just drop the seeking but it always pops up again trying to convince me to try some new strategy. There just never seems to be lasting relief anywhere I look or with whatever I try.

"... Either I am the bodymind and the world is real or the world is not real and just a reflection of a self-aware no thing that has no qualities or attributes" sounds to me like you're juggling two concepts about what you might be, but neither one gets at a feeling-belief about what you are. We climb Jacob's ladder of self-definition by losing identification with feeling-beliefs. Belief in being the visible/felt body can be dislodged when we "see" that we're that which experiences, and the body is an experience. But belief that we're something whose existence depends on the body can only be dislodged if we "become" that which is the source of consciousness.

For a logical/intellectual seeker, the progression is likely to be from the starting point of believing we're the body to believing we're the thinker, to believing we're the decision-maker and other mental processes. Each of those steps is likely to be a discontinuity or satori-type experience.

Seeking is the symptom of dissatisfaction, not the problem. Our hope lies in seeking. And successes come through repeated disillusionments, some of which may feel like failures. All progress comes by a broadening of what we see/intuit. Eventually we reach a point where our direction reverses from the long backing-away-from-untruth, and we're pulled through the door into absolute knowing. That knowing is radically different from the mind's familiar types of knowing, and it settles the mind's existential concerns.

There is no absolute subject… what Is, is absolute being. We become it and recognize the mind and its cosmos as our projection.

Are you familiar with *Pathways Through to Space* by Franklin Merrell-Wolff?

Ha! I used to be somewhat of a perfectionist, too, but these days I'm happy settling for mediocrity.

Being on fire is overrated. Better to simmer over an extended period, like chickpeas cooking in a pot (as Rumi astutely called his students, figuratively anyway).

Your identity can only be J. if you're identified with what you're seeing/experiencing. In this topsy-turvy world, we are precisely the opposite of that which we, the experiencer, experience.

We feel love for that which we are identified with. Ergo, self-love when we're identified with a life-story we're experiencing... with occasional pressure-release when we fall in love with a mate or a child or an ideal.

Problems arise to the degree that we try to control our lives. We try to control our lives to the degree that we're lost in the life-story that we're watching. Zazen, if it's simply watching the mind, will give us some detachment from what we're watching.

Are you familiar with the book *The Answer to How is Yes* by Peter Block? I remember that Shawn Nevins was impressed with it a few years back, and he mentioned it again recently, so I just got it from the local library yesterday to take a look. From the first few pages I've read, he's got a good line on how the desire to control is a suboptimal way to live a meaningful life.

As Rose said, "You learn sooner or later that you are not running the show and that if you relax, the show runs better."

The question that Block suggests to replace the "How?" question is: "What matters?" Matters to me, not to society. It's really another way of asking ourselves what our values are, and then honoring them.

Relax. Smile :-)

[Dear reader: You can undoubtedly pick up the gist of the email I was responding to, which I have omitted for reasons of privacy.]

❧

Naw, that "not sure I want it enough" stuff and "reluctance to surrender" are just stories that J's left hemisphere fabricates.

What provides movement inward is when the mind "sees" two conflicting "pictures" of what it believes itself to be. It stares long enough at those contestants to determine which one is relatively more true. We don't talk ourselves into inward movement.

"I am a separate entity" isn't yet a clear picture of that belief. Instead of telling stories about it, drill into it... What does "entity" really mean, or look like, to you?

What prevents movement inward is fear. Fear is the antipathy of love. At the decision-making level, feelings (desires and fears) are an integral part of the necessary data. In many ways it's an emotional process. The intuition, which functions at a higher-level, processes ("sees") feelings as well as thoughts but does not get caught up in them.

Regarding "the little man at the control panel is in a hall of mirrors, so there is a never-ending loop of watcher watching the watcher" — what do you feel that little guy is doing? Is it the separate entity you feel yourself to be?

[Dear reader: Another example of responding to correspondence I haven't shown you. This was not from the same J. as the previous one.]

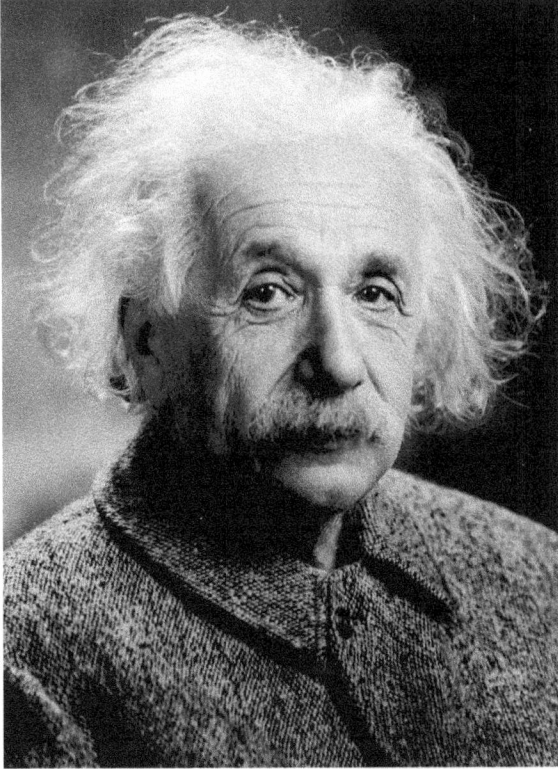

Albert Einstein (1879-1955)
A seeker of the absolute beyond relativity?
1947 photograph by Orren Jack Turner, Princeton, N.J.

"The River"

The Ohio River flows
along where I walk most days.
It begins in Pittsburgh,
formed by the confluence

of two rivers there,
then meanders for nearly
a thousand miles
before flowing into the

Mississippi, which in turn
flows for about another
eleven hundred miles before
merging into the ocean.

What is a river?
Without the water
it is a dry abstraction,
a mere concept.

A river with no water:
no-river.
A mind with no thought:
no-mind.

About the Author

In the spring of 1978, I met a man, Richard Rose, who awoke the sleeping intuition in me. For a dozen years since graduating from college I had experienced recurrent identity crises, feeling that I had everything that should have made me happy and yet there was some missing purpose or meaning in my life. Rose somehow got across the realization that I'd always been looking in the wrong direction, that all the answers to what I'd been looking for lay *within*. What I had been searching for was self-realization… and that wasn't going to be found outside.

In the fall of 1978, I documented my first attempt at verbalizing a commitment regarding my search: "Work with others now, and devote my life to helping others if I'm successful." I also noted that "there seems to have been a voice in me which has been saying for a long time: 'Define me, find me.'"

I pursued that goal rather relentlessly if not intelligently for a quarter century and found what I was looking for in 2004. Along the way I pretty much stuck to my commitment of working with others and continue to do so. I can't say with any certainty what, if anything, I did that either helped or hindered my search. And likewise I don't know with certainty what will help or hinder another person's search. Our intuition guides us, and intuition registers a downward current that comes into the mind from the source of awareness. The feeling-sense of the message coming from the light of awareness is that of nostalgia, calling us home.

Of this I'm rather sure: intentional commitment—scary as it may seem—opens doors magically. As Francis Thompson wrote in his poignant *Hound of Heaven,* we're designed to be able to return Home while living if we sincerely desire that.

🌿

See *SelfDiscoveryPortal.com* for more material and contact info.

Graphics Credits

Cover photo and/or front end paper: Atlantic Ocean from Dún Aonghus cliff, Inis Mór (Aran Islands). By the author.

Mohiniyattam dance performance (p. 13): Wikimedia Commons.

Bankei's *ensō:* **The Unborn Buddha Mind** *(p. 35): Painted by the Rinzai Zen master Bankei Yōtaku (1622-1693).*

Walt Whitman at home in Camden, NJ 1891 *(p. 62): Wikimedia Commons.*

Downtown Moundsville, WV *(p. 87): Wikimedia Commons.*

Sacred ivy, painted by Corina Baldasuc *(p. 113): Thanks to Corina. Also used for the cover of the "Meetings with Remarkable Women" DVD produced by www.PoetryInMotionFilms.com.*

Atlantic shore, USA *(p. 141): Thanks to www.edupic.net – free photographs and graphics for education.*

Albert Einstein *(p. 161): 1947 Wikimedia Commons photograph by Orren Jack Turner.*

Author *(p. 163): 2019 photograph by Tess Hughes.*

�֍

Your Love

God's will is whatever happens. It's the collapsing of the probability wave in quantum physics. Reunion with the Source may not be god's will for all creatures. Not all buds on an apple tree flower....

Acceptance relates to the past and present, not some imaginary future. In all honesty, how can you pretend to know one way or the other what's in store for that lovable bud that you're watching and identified with (in love with because, in fact, you are its source).

If the flower bud is self-conscious, it may feel that it's struggling to open. How poignant would that be, looking at what you've created and knowing that it's struggling to find Your Love, which has never left it.

❧

Define Me, Find Me

Would a moment of Pure Love that immolates you in its flame of union be more desirable than an eternity of safety?

Afterword

A good amount of time has passed since I put this book together. Going through it, I have made only a few minor edits. There were some exchanges about the concept of our sense of self, but I'd like to say a little more about it.

When someone asks us if we're awake (or we ask ourselves), the mind-self is able to "look back" and sense itself: "Yes, I'm here." Around 18 months of age, we begin to show evidence of self-awareness. Psychologists test that development with a "rouge test": they put a red mark on the toddler's nose to see what will happen when the toddler sees his image in the mirror. And by age 2, toddlers will touch their own noses where they see the reflection of the red mark.

What about dogs? Do they have a sense of self? Do ants? Acorns? Mark-tests similar to the toddler rouge-tests have been done with a variety of animals, who are marked on a spot they cannot normally see (often under anesthesia) and then given access to a mirror. If they then touch or investigate the mark, it indicates they recognize the image in the mirror as themselves. Dolphins, chimpanzees, and magpies often pass the mirror self-recognition test. Even ants have passed the test. Dogs, however, have not. But they do show self-recognition of their odor compared with the odors of other dogs in "sniff tests" of self-recognition.

No one has designed a test yet for acorns or oak trees. But plants can sense, learn, remember and act in ways similar to animals. Although they don't have nerve cells, they can send electrical signals and even produce neurotransmitters like the human brain uses.

As children age, they adopt many beliefs about the self they can sense. By age 3 we have a complete way of viewing ourselves as child versus adult, boy versus girl, good versus bad, etc., when asked. Young children can also describe themselves in simple emotional terms, such as: "Today, I'm happy. I like to play with Toby."

On the horns of a dilemma... The sense of self sits on the fence between being the unknown *subject* "us" that we're looking for and an *object* in our consciousness. It is paradoxical, and we tend to feel we're at the end of the line when we hit a paradox, so we drop it. But there's another approach, which is to let it become a koan—which doesn't yield to reason, but we can let the mind try to feel its way into it or beyond it.

❧

Believe in Me

Listen to the sound of silence:

Struggling blindly in the fog of beliefs, you grasp first one then another in the quest for security.

What you seek lies between and behind these beliefs. I am the respectful doubt, the solvent that detaches beliefs.

Believe in me.

Doubt combined with faith doesn't lead to nihilism. It is the royal path to Certainty.

I am.

Art Ticknor never was... he existed and still exists as a ray of me, an ephemeron.

Only I am.

Other Titles from TAT Foundation Press

Hydroglyphics: Reflections on the Sacred
by Phaedra Greenwood and Shawn Nevins

Falling For Truth: A Spiritual Death And Awakening
by Howdie Mickoski

Awake at the Wheel: Norio Kushi's Highway Adventures and the Unmasking of the Phantom Self by Stephen Earle

Subtraction: The Simple Math of Enlightenment
by Shawn Nevins

This Above All: A Journey of Self-Discovery
by Tess Hughes

A Handyman's Common Sense Guide to Spiritual Seeking
by David Weimer

At Home with the Inner Self
by Jim Burns

Beyond Mind, Beyond Death

Beyond Relativity by Art Ticknor

The Celibate Seeker by Shawn Nevins

Images of Essence by Bob Fergeson and Shawn Nevins

The Listening Attention by Bob Fergeson

The Perennial Way: New English versions of Yoga Sutras, Dhammapada, Heart Sutra, Ashtavakra Gita, Faith Mind Sutra, and Tao Te Ching by Bart Marshall

Solid Ground of Being by Art Ticknor

For more information on the TAT Foundation visit tatfoundation.org.